Flea Market *Flair*

FRESH IDEAS FOR VINTAGE FINDS

LISA MARIE HART

CENTENNIAL BOOKS

Flea Market *Flair*

contents

62

174

CHAPTER 3
MAKE IT YOURS

88

The Wonderful World of Flea Market Finds!

Whether you're searching for a bargain, filling out a collection or out for a day's entertainment, there's much to discover when you're browsing through vintage.

What gives us a greater sense of anticipation for the thrill of the hunt than getting ready for a day of bargain-shopping and making a beeline for a vintage market that's bursting into the aisles with untapped treasures?

Whether inside or out, winter, spring, summer or fall, vintage and flea markets not only provide an exciting way to spend a day—poring over the possibilities, inspecting those with potential and selecting our favorite new finds to bring home with us—but they also shape the foundation of an authentically collected home. (And we all know: That's the best kind of home there is!)

Those objects and furnishings have a story (or two) behind each one. And even if those stories never reveal themselves, they offer a very real connection to the past in a meaningful way that defies practical explanation. We somehow feel as if we have "known" these items somewhere before. And their presence soon adds a layer to our lives that seems nearly impossible to live without.

These beautiful, mysterious artifacts enter our spaces in the same way they fill up the flea: one by one. Human hearts pluck them from wherever they were, detecting a glint of something special, a quality they believe other like-minded souls will see in them, too. Human hands bring every individual item together in a haul they deliver, with significant effort, to the market just for us.

While we may think of flea markets as stretching only as far back as our first memory of strolling through one as a wide-eyed child, marketplaces have been a cultural necessity turned phenomenon since the origins of ancient civilizations. Historians say these markets first popped up in the U.S. in Texas

in the 1870s. Now, there are an estimated 5,000 nationwide, stocked by over a million entrepreneurial vendors and shopped by 100 million grateful guests.

More than mere shopping, flea markets represent a communal meeting of kindred spirits. You can find yourself across the country and still feel at home among the local sellers and their stalls. They are places of sentiment, wonder and comforting familiarity.

This book, in turn, was assembled with great care, designed as a destination rich in variety and deep with ideas to stir up one's own personal style. Our goal is to offer up fresh ideas for collecting, displaying, decorating and DIY-ing, with pages you'll revisit time and time again, catching something new on each occasion.

We cover what to expect from the modern market scene, how to bargain, how to uncover the best stuff, when to go, when to splurge and when to keep on walking. Then, you'll learn how to adorn your biggest walls, clean and care for the most delicate of vintage linens and create a home work area that doesn't feel like another day at the office. You'll also find an in-depth look at a dozen spectacular abodes, including several abroad, that transcend style labels. Learn the history behind each one, plus easy tips, clever tricks and savvy techniques the owners used to make them special. And stoke the fires of project inspiration, from how to give old furniture a stunning makeover to upcycling and repurposing even basic finds into creative showpieces you'll love.

Ever-evolving flea markets are a pleasure, a pastime and a passion many of us were fortunate to have passed down to us. It's only natural that we are moved to pass the tradition onto others. Share this book with someone you love, and keep the circle of flea market love alive!

—*Lisa Marie Hart*

FIND AND SEEK
You never know what treasures will end up being part of your home after you visit a flea market!

CHAPTER 1

VINTAGE LOVE

When a home is filled with old stuff, the heart beats with delight.

Anatomy of a Modern Market

These events have seriously upped their game. More personal, interactive and styled than ever, junking markets of the moment are full-blown celebrations of a lifelong commitment to vintage love.

Market Beautiful's event takes over Montana's Big Mountain Ranch.

LOCAL COLOR
Scenic or unusual locations, from bucolic farms to urban playgrounds

TIME TO GO
Tiered admission charges for different days and times. VIP, pre-entry preview parties, and night-before events offer early shopping perks, as do early-bird admission tickets (sometimes before 5 a.m.!)

NOM NOM
Food and dessert trucks, specialty cuisine (from sushi to gluten-free) and chef demos. Pricey water!

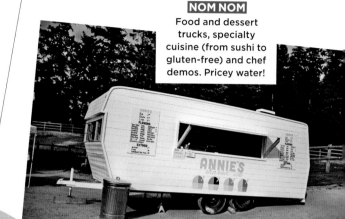

PUPS OK
Pet-friendly markets, some with dog-cart rentals

IF YOU'VE DUCKED OUT OF THE FLEA MARKET SCENE, HERE'S WHAT YOU'VE BEEN MISSING...

FARM FRESH
Farmers markets with artisan baked goods, honey, soap, candles, plants and fresh flowers

TRANSPORTIVE
Rentals of electric scooters to get around on, and rolling hand carts to get your load to the car—plus door-to-door delivery service

LISTEN UP
Guest speakers (even folks from HGTV!) and meet-and-greets

LET'S CONNECT
Vintage fashion shows and photo booths to show off your new (old) stuff. On-site workshops, from hand lettering to potting succulent gardens

PLAYTIME
Family activities such as lawn games, kids' crafting tables, face painting, climbing walls, bounce houses, balloon art, petting zoos, pony rides and bonfires. Day-to-night live music and dancing

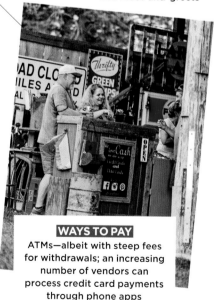

DRINK UP
Craft beer; beer gardens; wine, scotch and whiskey tastings; gourmet coffee bars

WAYS TO PAY
ATMs—albeit with steep fees for withdrawals; an increasing number of vendors can process credit card payments through phone apps

11

Should I...?

A pair of seasoned sellers weigh in on your big-ticket questions.

Who knows the ins and outs of market shopping better than two friends who founded a multilocation market? In 2011, Coley Arnold and Lindsey Holt accidentally sparked a thrifting sensation. "We were hoarders and needed to clear out our garages," Holt says, laughing. "Twenty-three vendors sold their stuff at our backyard sale, and 600 people spent $15,000 in four hours!" Both women, each the mom of three

If you hit the flea market intending to window-shop, you're bound to score the biggest haul. Rent a truck to avoid missing out.

More than 100 vendors bring their chipped, rusty, vintage and handmade wares to the Junk in the Trunk Vintage Markets.

kids, agree: They weren't looking to start a business. "But people were knocking down our doors, asking for the next sale," Arnold explains. Their Junk in the Trunk Vintage Market events now pop up in Southern California and Arizona, blending vendors with live music and food trucks for a family-friendly atmosphere. Here, their insider's take on shopping like a pro... (For more on their markets, see page 42.)

Should I take an Uber to the flea market?
We would avoid it. Most people who say they're just coming to look around don't stick to that. About 99 percent walk out with something. You don't want to be stuck not being able to get it home or regret not being able to buy that fab find. (**Author's note:** If you're dedicated to shopping solely for vintage tablecloths and pillowcases or a few Bakelite bangles, experiment once to see if your plan works. We will all admire your willpower.)

Should I pay extra for early entry?
Absolutely! Vendors usually have only one of every piece—that's why you shop vintage! Early birds catch the best junk. A lot of our shoppers don't like crowds, so our markets offer an early-shopping experience for the first hour on Saturday morning and a relaxed VIP night on Friday. People come early to sip a glass of wine, listen to music and browse without stress. (They also get first dibs on all the good stuff!) Friday is a completely different feel. Vendors restock for Saturday, so shoppers come back to see what's new. Some even come again Sunday afternoon, when vendors are willing to wheel and deal to prevent hauling stuff home. It all depends on what kind of shopper you are.

Should I ask about having something shipped or delivered to my door?
It's worth asking. But most vendors want to get rid of their merchandise right away, and that gives you bargaining power. If you take it home yourself, most will give 10 percent off. Bring measurements of your spaces and rent a U-Haul or a truck. It never fails: There is *always* someone at our markets who buys a set of lockers, then tries to shove them into a Prius. Don't be that person! Also, apps that arrange delivery of bulky items are coming on the scene, so check in advance to see if this service is offered in your area.

13

Work It

No matter your style, find key pieces
that will help your home office stand out.

Farmhouse Fresh

White + soft
neutrals promote
peace and clarity

1 Open compartments on a vintage desk appeal to
messy-but-organized types. **2** Vintage rulers fill a cream
pitcher, part of the ironstone collection from Melissa
Urban of the blog Shabby Love. **3** Erin Kern of cottonstem.
com runs her interiors business from a tiny "she shed."
Inside, this curvy French desk and chair meet more modern
farmhouse elements in a cozy space that lets creativity
flow. **4** Liz Fourez of lovegrowswild.com fills her home,
and home office, with easy DIY projects.

Two desks form an L shape in DIYer Jessica Wasserman's rosy office.

The farmhouse look favors laidback, rustic-meets-industrial styles characterized by natural textures and materials like iron, steel and galvanized metal.

Midcentury Modern

Sleek design from the 1950s–1970s creates an air of distinction

1 A 1970s Tenson adjustable task lamp personifies the reasons the '70s are coming back: It's big and straightforward, and it gives a bit of glitz with the gold-tone arm. **2** For the home of a young family, Carole Marcotte of Form & Function in Raleigh, North Carolina, designed this desk/craft area in the son's bedroom. She used a door for the writing surface. Shelves display a vintage globe collection, and an aqua molded chair on wheels ties into the hue. **3** Made from solid oak, this angled desk-organizer caddy was manufactured in the 1950s by the renowned Globe–Wernicke company. The sturdy little cabinets and files were built for industry. **4** The two-tiered construction of this mod wooden desk makes the upper storage portion appear to float above the workspace.

"Be steady and well-ordered in your life so that you can be fierce and original in your work."

Gustave Flaubert

Midcentury looks have a retro edge that still feels cool today.

Midcentury pieces excel in simple, attractive functionality. This minimalist desk, chair and gooseneck task lamp set from the 1960s is a perfect example. Modest yet good-looking, the small desk has a durable metal frame, two drawers and an easy-to-clean Formica top. The molded-back chair boasts a padded green vinyl seat.

Classic Antique

Get inspired by furnishings and accents from eras past

1 The smallest corner and oldest desk can make an inviting place to work if graced by natural light. Add artwork, flowers and a cup of sharpened pencils. **2** Quaint vintage paperweights provide desktop charm. **3** Start with a desk you love. Even if you have to splurge, a carved antique wood desk like this does wonders for atmosphere and state of mind. **4** Wall shelving lets this office double as a display room for antique collectibles.

Bathe your space with light from
multiple sources. Put lighting on
a dimmer or use three-way bulbs.
Table lamps shine more softly
than traditional desk lamps.

Don't forget
to add photos
of loved ones
to keep you
smiling!

Ideas for Large Walls

Why go bare when you can go big? Borrow these impactful ideas from emerging artists, established bloggers and creative DIYers.

1

Sixteen tennis rackets make one big bloom on a dark wall.

1 Tennis Rackets

Kem Theilig of IN:SITE Design Build Associates of San Francisco created serious flower power for her home office in Palm Springs, California. Set in the historic Tennis Club neighborhood, the home and its location represent her love of the game.

2 Hats

The talented Lee Vosburgh of stylebee.ca heads up an online hub for women around the world who seek to simplify their style and establish wardrobe contentment. A hat wall in her office speaks to her timeless personal taste.

2

I shall be miserable if I have not an excellent library

JANE AUSTEN
Pride & Prejudice

3

Flaunt your love of literature with books open to favorite passages.

3 Mirrors

A mural of stunning antique mirrors solves a pair of dilemmas: how to decorate a wall while reflecting light, and what to do when you stumble across a beautiful mirror but don't need one or have a place for it. Problems solved!

4 Open Books

Erin Kern of cottonstem.com created a viral sensation with this DIY installation. "Every time we close the last page of a book, we are better for it," she says. "This pays tribute to some of the stories that shaped the story of me...just needed a hammer and nails."

1 Purses

If your pretty vintage purses are anywhere but hanging on a wall for all to admire, you may be missing a chance for home décor greatness. As a bonus, you'll find it much easier to select one that matches your dress!

Pick a purse for tonight's dinner date— no digging required.

2 Big Art

Susan Daggett of kindredvintage.com chose a wood-framed art print as a focal point for the space, then added a sitting area. Entitled *Darling*, the piece is designed and hand-lettered by artist Aedriel Moxley.

Every beautiful collection deserves a place to see and be seen.

3 Plates
Kristi Dominguez of ishouldbemoppingthefloor.com hangs vintage church plates to define her dining room corner.

4 Clocks
They don't have to show the correct time—or even be in working order—to tell a story. Timepieces from past eras are workaday works of art.

5 Family Photos
Along her stairway, DIYer Jessica Wasserman hung a mix of black-and-white and color prints in an assortment of frame sizes, colors and shapes, with art and beloved collectibles mixed in for variety and sentimental value.

6 Hoops
Erin Kern of cottonstem.com used embroidery hoops, greenery and twine to soften her DIY shiplap bed frame.

1 Your Own Paintings

Artist Mary-Catheryn Baker of Copper Corners layers an ever-changing gallery of her freshly dried artwork over a patterned wall in her studio, then rotates in fresh pieces.

2 Saws

Taking these from rusted to reused, the resourceful DIYer Katrina Lounsbury collected a series of old, wedge-shaped handsaws to make this primitive daisy on the side of her garden shed. She attached part of a small chicken feeder to serve as its center.

3 Books

A mere wall becomes a library, a place to get lost in, with the addition of simple shelving for books. Pair it with a comfy chair, and you'll be more apt to make time to enjoy them.

4 Botanical Prints

This Southern-charm bedroom is by interior designer Ashley Gilbreath of Montgomery, Alabama. Above the ivory spindle bed, framed botanical prints in both an uneven number and asymmetrical arrangement add interest.

5 Flowers

The whimsical look of a ladder suspended in the air, trailing faux flowers and greenery that seem to grow from its rungs is enchanting. Erin Kern of cottonstem.com sourced the chipping old ladder at a local flea market to hang above her potting station.

6 Footboard

A painted cottage prairie piece turns antique footboards into unique handmade coat racks.

From baby dresses to ballet slippers, hang them on hooks as décor.

For the Love of Linens

Line-dried-fresh tips for laundering, pressing, displaying and using these enduring pieces of history.

Pair your vintage floral tablecloths with teacup "vases" on a saucer.

2

"The breeze catches the sheets…. I pull up the covers and smell the sunshine."

Constance Anderson, author of *Smelling Sunshine*

3

Many of us recall a peaceful summer night's sleep at our grandparents' house, absolutely cool, comfortable and content between a fresh set of sheets. Crisp and wonderfully scented, the sheets had been dried in the sun, billowing lightly in the breeze from their wooden clothespins on the laundry line all afternoon. The way those sheets smelled and felt against our skin made us feel so cared for—like all was right with the world.

Vintage linens have a way of transporting us back in time—even to a time period we have never experienced. It's no wonder that flea market stalls piled high with brightly printed cotton tablecloths, starched napkins, embroidered pillowcases, barkcloth curtains and dainty hankies, as well as aprons with pockets and trailing ties, are often as full of shoppers as they are linens!

For every customer who buys them and enjoys them (yay, you!), there is another right behind her who is guilty of purchasing a perfectly pressed set of linens only to put them away, for fear that she will never be able to re-create their pristine condition.

A few tricks of the trade are all it takes to keep your finds looking antiques shop–lovely. And while linens don't need to be high-maintenance and fussy, we've collected some tips for buying and taking care of them at a level that matches your style.

1 A vintage scallop-edged quilt makes a romantic layer when folded on a sofa. **2** Embroidery on this tablecloth complements a Royal Albert china teacup and saucer in the American Beauty pattern. **3** Simplicity is always in style: Vintage silver and linens are a timeless pairing.

vintage fabrics were manufactured to last. Cotton, linen and damask are surprisingly durable.

3 **Treat and Soak** Stains are the nemesis of vintage fabric. Caused by any number of culprits, they may taint the fibers for decades before someone decides to remove them. Even so, many will relax and give way after a long, rehydrating soak in the tub (just like humans do!).

For fine linens, generally soiled fabric, or pieces with lace, fringe or crocheted trim, presoak for 15 minutes in clear warm water to loosen and remove dirt and old detergents before laundering. Severely discolored fabrics may need to soak 24 to 48 hours or longer. Don't give up: Soaking has worked its share of textile miracles.

If linens are yellowed, use a scoop of OxiClean (a chlorine-free cleaning agent of hydrogen peroxide and a sodium compound) in a tub of warm water. (Some say hotter is better, but that is debatable.)

1 **Select** Unfold and examine linens carefully on both sides before buying. (They may be displayed or folded in a way that hides their flaws.) Gauge the fabric's strength by giving it a gentle tug. Hold it up to the light with an eye for stains, rips, tears or thinning areas that may soon wear into a hole. Despite your best efforts, some stains may not come out. Purchase for a price you can live with if they don't, or leave them for the next linen lover.

2 **Assess** Generally speaking, the older the fabric, the more delicate and susceptible to further damage—even from water or by cleaning. Some, such as highly sentimental heritage fabrics, may need to be cleaned by an antiques expert or professional restorer. Your dry cleaner may accept antique pieces but will likely add a disclaimer, since there is always a risk in dry-cleaning or laundering an heirloom. Curtains, barkcloth and heavy bedding (aside from chenille, which can be machine-washed and dried) are also on the dry-cleaning drop-off list. The same goes for fabrics that are musty, mildewed, or dry and brittle. Test embroidered items for colorfastness by blotting threads lightly with a damp white cloth or paper towel. If the color bleeds off, it will need to be dry-cleaned. The rest of your linens may be safe to launder. While it's always wise to err on the side of caution and begin with a simple soak, many

For a more eclectic look, try mixing and matching flatware.

1 A vintage quilt invites picnics in the park. **2** Open shelving is the perfect place to show off small linens. **3** Turn your square tablecloth for a country-casual look.

Transform tea towels into a valance by turning them lengthwise and using clips to hang them from curtain rings.

3

This bed crown, with new or vintage fabric, creates a canopy effect that emphasizes the room's height.

1

You can also add a scoop of a stain fighter like Biz for even more cleaning power. Gently agitate, knead the fabric like dough (do not rub), then soak overnight. Rinse with cold water (then, optionally, with vinegar). Never use bleach, which is simply too harsh.

To "bleach" white fabrics the old-fashioned way, rub a mixture of lemon juice and salt over the stain and then lay them out to dry in the sun. Rinse well and let dry again.

For rust stains, try a solvent called Whink. Engleside's Restoration Fabric Restorer also has a reputation for purging stains when all else fails.

4 Launder Before our top-loading, energy-efficient machines, linens were washed by hand—and that remains the safest bet for preserving them. Dissolve a mild, nonabrasive detergent in hot water and then let it cool to tepid before adding fabric, swishing around and working it into the water. Ivory Snow, Dreft and Woolite have long been used for laundering vintage linens, but newer, natural, phosphate-free soaps are also good choices. To boost the clean factor, Borax All Natural Laundry Booster, Biz or OxiClean are fan favorites. Fels-Naptha can be used on light stains at this step; knead the fabric together to work in. Soak for several hours or, ideally, overnight before rinsing at least twice in clear, cool water to get rid of all soap residue. Soak longer, if needed; extra rinses are always better. Launder immediately after using to keep new stains from setting in.

5 Dry Do not wring out. Instead, gently roll each piece in a clean, white towel to absorb excess water or simply press it onto a towel (or press between two towels) to blot dry. If you don't have a clothesline, place a portable drying rack in the sun. You can use two, spaced apart, to hang sheets or large tablecloths. Some collectors swear by another method: Lay linens flat on a white towel or sheet—or even directly on the grass—to dry in the sun. Air-drying is always recommended; the lowest delicate or fluff (no heat) setting on your dryer may work on heartier fabrics, in a pinch. Remove linens immediately and shake.

6 Iron Press with a dry iron while still damp. This is especially key to smoothing pieces with embroidery, which should always be ironed

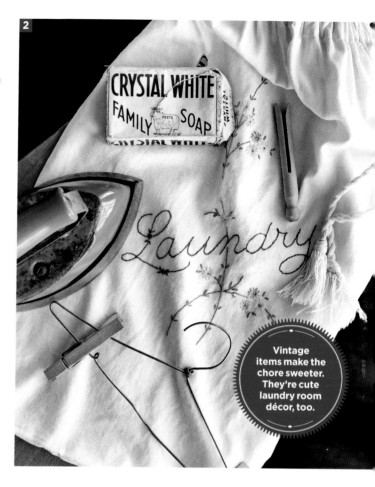

Vintage items make the chore sweeter. They're cute laundry room décor, too.

from the reverse side with a towel underneath. Work in small sections, starting from the backside and followed by the front. Iron back and forth with the weave, since circular motions can stretch the cloth. Heavy or liquid starch will add refinement.

Some experts suggest waiting to iron fabrics until you're ready to use them, but everyone has his or her own methods. If a tablecloth has wrinkles, place it, with a couple of damp towels, in the dryer on low heat for a few minutes. Remove it while it's still warm and smooth. You can iron a tablecloth right on the table, if you place a sheet underneath. Using medium heat, move the iron quickly and pull and smooth as you go. Those who like to iron their sheets can press just the folded-over top sheet once the bed is made—if ironing them on an ironing board when damp seems too daunting.

1 A fresh white coverlet balances a room of red toile.
2 These charming bygone relics belong to Melanie Butcher of @vintagecharmhouse on Instagram.

Best of Both Worlds

Seven secrets for mingling old and new in one timeless room.

If you've been wondering if you can really have it all under one roof, the answer is yes! Consider the modest space pictured at right, which carries the light look of springtime, dotted with flea market finds that never need to be put away: A contemporary geometric rug can indeed find a happy home with vintage linens and enamelware. Whether your rooms have started to sag under the heaviness of too many antiques or your contemporary décor could use a splash of authentic vintage charm, try these seven easy tips to beautify one nook or your whole home.

1 Do the Math Not to sound calculating, but most people find an old-new formula they're comfortable with, and they stick with it. Those who lean modern usually mix 75 percent new pieces with 25 percent vintage accents. Those with a soft spot for vintage might opt for a 50/50 ratio, placing an old Colonial or farmhouse table as a centerpiece instead of the clean-lined sawhorse table used in this dining area, which feels more of-the-moment.

2 Nature Nurtures Spaces filled with natural light, natural textures and references to Mother Nature's world around us make everyone feel right at home. This room brings the outdoors in with cottage floral prints, an art print of plants and tiny critters and whitewashed shiplap walls. (If big prints on pillows and place mats feel too bold, look for textiles that reverse to solids.)

3 Be a Schemer One of the most classic retro color pairings is a deep lipstick red tempered by a soft mint green or pastel turquoise. Call it robin red and duck-egg blue or candy apple and pale aqua, this lively, old-fashioned duo can feel as 1950s kitschy or as current as you choose. Base your scheme off a pillow, a piece of art, mismatched chairs or an heirloom tablecloth and build around it.

4 Tap Into Nostalgia Recall your best childhood memories and find a way to incorporate them. Mason-jar pendant lights hang above this table like fireflies in two jars. Pull a relic from your past and give it a place to shine. If your parents or grandparents had an eye-catching collectible you always admired, chances are you can find something similar in the markets or on eBay to rekindle the memory in your own surroundings.

5 Make Some Flower Power Keep vases of staggering heights on the table and refill them weekly with cuttings and seasonal flowers. (We love this mix of glass with an oversize enamel pitcher.) If you don't have blooms to pick outside your window, buy one large arrangement and divide it into several bunches. Snip a bit of greenery to fill in the gaps.

6 Go Double Duty Make a small space more multifunctional by adding a shelving unit that houses handled wooden crates you can pull out for different activities. From the kids' homework and science-fair projects to your own crafts, gift wrapping and decorating, the crates keep supplies organized and handy while exuding vintage appeal.

7 Treat Yourself Like a Guest The best décor means little if you never take time out to enjoy what you've created. Make time for afternoon tea (or whatever else you may fancy) and serve it in a teapot at the table, rather than taking it straight from a kettle.

A geometric rug stays on trend, paired with vintage flair.

The World Is a Flea

You need these far-flung markets in your life—or at least on your travel radar.

Marchés, markets and souks draw millions of shoppers every year. While the merits of the world's most famous (and famously large) flea markets have been debated (only adding to their hype), even gloomy weather and pressing crowds never fail to deter those who have a yen to experience these international phenoms. It's easy to surrender any formal plans in favor of meandering aimlessly through the colorful rows of vintage and antique vestiges that reflect the region's culture. Don't count on any bargains, but a day at the market can be just as enriching as one at a nearby museum. Chances are, you'll return home with an urge to infuse a bit of the local décor style into your own sacred spaces.

Founded in a converted Danish post office in 1775, Royal Copenhagen is known for its European-style blue-and-white porcelain.

The Look

Danes speak English very well, but if you would ike to thank a vendor in Danish, say: *Tak skal du have!*

The open-air markets of Old Copenhagen are a cultural treat, not only for their high-quality items but also for the surrounding architecture.

THORVALDSENS PLADS ANTIQUE MARKET
Copenhagen, Denmark

Centrally located in the scenic heart of the Old Copenhagen Quarter, next to the Thorvaldsens Museum, this modest-sized market puts quality above quantity. Tables of beautiful vintage and antique items invite a Friday or Saturday stroll. In a city known for its seasonal secondhand markets, this one is considered a must-shop. It's open from the end of April through the end of October.

• **The Look** Well-designed environments with clean lines, select vintage pieces and a modern edge. Warm woods meet cool crisp whites in a smartly tranquil setting. A burst of color is optional.

• **Shop For** Finely crafted midcentury furnishings and accessories made of teak or rosewood, vintage Royal Copenhagen porcelain, Danish ceramics and elegant design objects.

• **Insider's Alternatives** **Veras Market** (a secondhand clothing market that pops up at indoor and outdoor locales all over the city); **Frederiksberg Flea Market** (locals love these 90 high-style stalls set in a posh neighborhood); **Nørrebro Loppemarked** (a unique vibe defines this long and narrow sidewalk flea market); and **Ravnsborggade Market** (held several times a year in the art, antique and designer district).

PORTOBELLO ROAD
London

You won't spot Queen Elizabeth II digging for royal treasures among Portobello's 1,000 merchants, then stopping to watch street performers or ducking into one of the pubs. But you will find an archive of commemorative souvenirs produced over the course of her decades-long reign—only part of what makes "the world's largest antiques market" so fascinating. What originated as a farmers market in the 800s has evolved into a modern-day extravaganza that still sells fruits, vegetables and foodstuffs along with LPs, movie posters, vintage clothing and myriad artifacts for Anglophiles. It's open daily in part; all sections, including the antiques arcade, are open on Saturdays.

• **The Look** A dark and moody London flat mirrors the local forecast. Urban yet homey, interiors range from bohemian to those with traditional formality. Londoners favor a bold, Brit pop of color (often red or yellow)—and don't mind a dash of wit.

• **Shop For** English china, Victorian jewelry and pocket watches, vintage cameras, silver serving pieces, British Army toys, vintage fashion, royal whatnots, old sports equipment, quirky collectibles.

• **Insider's Alternatives** **Greenwich Market** (for street food, local artisans and antique furniture); **Brick Lane Market** (a lively Sunday scene of vintage clothing, secondhand goods and ethnic restaurants); and **Alfies Antique Market** (four floors of fashion, jewelry, art and homewares).

Culinary delights to fuel your Portobello hunt include falafel, bratwurst, curry, paella and crepes.

You never know what you'll find along Portobello Road—and that's half the fun. A long-eared dog needs a good home too, don't you think?

Tidy and organized are *not* prerequisites for vendors at the world's largest antiques market. Come prepared to dig for buried treasure.

Decorative painted serving dishes, platters and bowls envelop a stall at The Souks, where the range of choices can seem almost overwhelming.

Aside from shopping, two must-do rituals are drinking mint tea and hand-washing with rosewater.

THE SOUKS

Marrakech, Morocco

Getting lost is just part of this crazy, labyrinthine shopping experience. Embrace the chaos of the sprawling maze and let your senses take in the aromatic spices, local delicacies, buzz of tourists, calls of eager vendors and vibrant handcrafted items that rise to the roof around every bend. Few markets in the world make such a stamp on one's memory. Bring an empty suitcase and consider a professional guide to lead you through the narrow alleyways full of donkeys, carts and motorbikes. It's open daily.

• **The Look** The exotic opulence of a sultan's tent defines this immersive style with the saturated colors of a Moroccan sunset: pink and orange, with glints of brass and gold. Lanterns (both strung and clustered on the floor), Berber carpets, carved wood tables and ornate pillows are key elements—everything is made by local hands, using techniques passed down through the ages.

• **Shop For** Rugs, textiles, brass, silver, lanterns, slippers, kaftans, fezzes, harem pants, leather goods, olives, teapots, tagine pots, spices, perfumes and jewel-toned tea glasses.

• **Insider's Alternatives Ensemble Artisanal** (a relaxed, high-quality arts and crafts complex with on-site makers); and the **Kasbah** (farther south and much less busy).

Hand-painted side tables with six or eight sides are the work of local artisans who favor rich colors and traditional designs.

The Look

The French admire fashion, so dress smartly and use French greetings while you shop.

MARCHÉ AUX PUCES
Paris

You can thank the French for naming our own shopping custom. This "market of the fleas" (also known as Les Puces de Saint-Ouen or Les Puces) lies along the north end of Paris in a jumble of open-air and covered markets. Don't be shy about pushing past the peddlers with less-desirable goods on the perimeter. With 1,700 merchants, there's no time for anything less than *très jolie*! Prices can be steep, so hold out for a heart-stopper: that one beautiful thing that feels oh-so-French. It's open Saturday through Monday.

• **The Look** An enveloping neutral canvas with period details in the architecture embodies the quintessential shabby-chic look called brocante. A Louis chair, an old birdcage and a chandelier make a fine start to a style that can lean French country or classic Parisian apartment.

• **Shop For** Scarves, jewelry, enamel kitchenware, hats, postcards, displayable books, charming paintings.

• **Insider's Alternatives Grande Braderie de Lille** (a festive weekend each September that dates to the 12th century); **Puces de Vanves** (a smaller market in the south end); and *vide-greniers* (annual sales where French villagers sell their wares together).

Small-group and private walking tours through Les Puces attract serious buyers.

Collectible vintage French matchbooks often have the allure of tiny works of art if you take the time to look.

More Must-Shop Markets

FERIA DE SAN TELMO
Buenos Aires, Argentina

This weekly street fair in a boho barrio has been going strong since 1971. Wear your walking shoes so you can take your time browsing the booths along 13 blocks of cobbled streets and historic architecture. Vintage clothing, antiques, leather goods and works by Argentine artisans are enhanced by local fare, tango dancers and other street performers. It's held every Sunday.

GRAND BAZAAR
Istanbul

Test your haggling skills inside one of the largest and oldest covered bazaars in the world. In existence since the 15th century, this bustling hub in Turkey's capital city is a gateway to the past. Explore 4,400 shops (over 61 streets with 18 gates) to find kilim bags, pashminas, carpets, silk clothes, copperware, evil eyes, lamps, ceramics, spices, pipes and Turkish delight candy. It's open daily except Sunday.

Great American Flea Markets

Considered the best of the best across the U.S., these epic events entice shoppers with loads of variety and unforgettable bargains.

Visit each market's website for current dates and details.

BYGONE GEMS IN NoCAL
Alameda Point Antiques Faire
Alameda, California, first Sunday of the month
Views of the San Francisco bridges, skyline and the mountains beyond envelop 800 booths at Northern California's largest flea market, where all items are at least 20 years old. Style-makers mark their calendars for the biannual Alameda Vintage Fashion Faire.
alamedapoint antiquesfaire.com

FUN FOR FAMILIES
Mile High Flea Market
Denver, Friday, Saturday and Sunday year-round
From the farmers market to the covered shops, live entertainment and kids' ride zone, there's something for everyone on "80 adventurous acres." Come often: It's open every weekend.
milehighfleamarket.com

A-LIST FAVORITE
Rose Bowl Flea Market
Pasadena, California, second Sunday of the month
Shoppers (including celebs in shades) arrive early for the best selection and mildest temperatures at this iconic flea, which has been going strong for more than a half century. Separate areas for new and vintage, home décor and clothing make it easy to target your efforts among the 2,500 vendors.
rgcshows.com/rose-bowl

STRICTLY VINTAGE
Long Beach Antique Market
Long Beach, California, third Sunday of the month
Scattered across 20 acres, this famed market with a reputation for quality is a bit smaller and more manageable than the Rose Bowl to the north. Vintage hounds can rest assured: The show's policy requiring merch to be more than 20 years old applies to all 800 stalls.
longbeachantiquemarket.com

DESERT DIVAS
Junk in the Trunk Vintage Market
California and Arizona, several times a year
Two best friends morphed a simple yard sale into a swanky, interactive concept. Their market locales guarantee an element of surprise every time. Highlights have included VIP Friday night preview parties, a moms' lounge, mural wall, kids' activity zone, outdoor games, beauty services in an Airstream trailer and a photo-booth bus.
junkinthetrunkvintage market.com

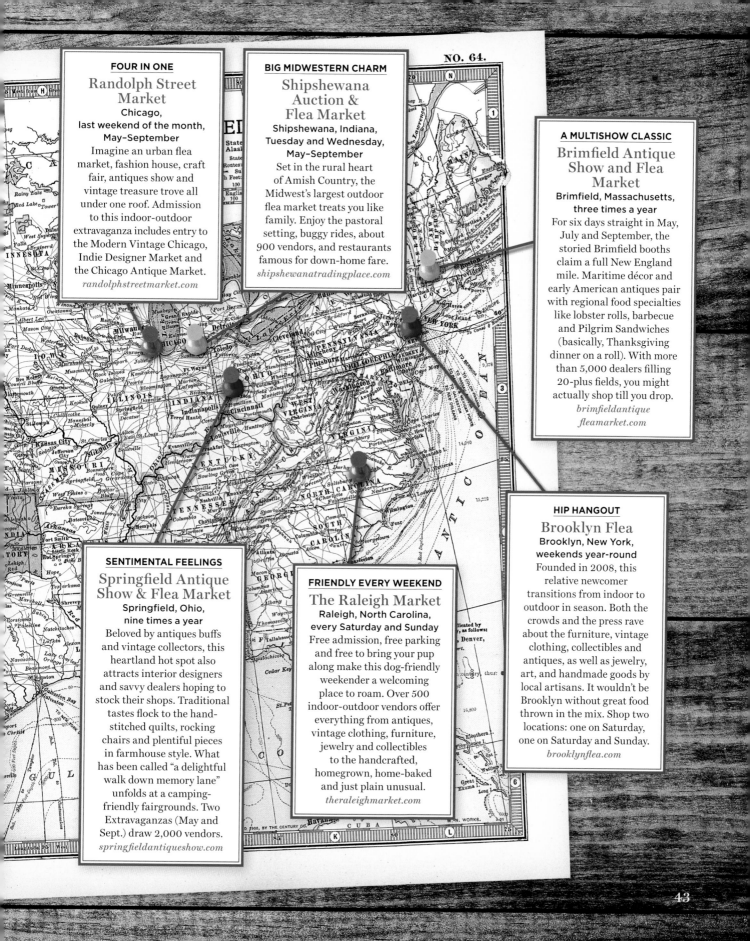

FOUR IN ONE
Randolph Street Market
**Chicago,
last weekend of the month,
May–September**

Imagine an urban flea market, fashion house, craft fair, antiques show and vintage treasure trove all under one roof. Admission to this indoor-outdoor extravaganza includes entry to the Modern Vintage Chicago, Indie Designer Market and the Chicago Antique Market.
randolphstreetmarket.com

BIG MIDWESTERN CHARM
Shipshewana Auction & Flea Market
**Shipshewana, Indiana,
Tuesday and Wednesday,
May–September**

Set in the rural heart of Amish Country, the Midwest's largest outdoor flea market treats you like family. Enjoy the pastoral setting, buggy rides, about 900 vendors, and restaurants famous for down-home fare.
shipshewanatradingplace.com

NO. 64.

A MULTISHOW CLASSIC
Brimfield Antique Show and Flea Market
**Brimfield, Massachusetts,
three times a year**

For six days straight in May, July and September, the storied Brimfield booths claim a full New England mile. Maritime décor and early American antiques pair with regional food specialties like lobster rolls, barbecue and Pilgrim Sandwiches (basically, Thanksgiving dinner on a roll). With more than 5,000 dealers filling 20-plus fields, you might actually shop till you drop.
brimfieldantique fleamarket.com

SENTIMENTAL FEELINGS
Springfield Antique Show & Flea Market
**Springfield, Ohio,
nine times a year**

Beloved by antiques buffs and vintage collectors, this heartland hot spot also attracts interior designers and savvy dealers hoping to stock their shops. Traditional tastes flock to the hand-stitched quilts, rocking chairs and plentiful pieces in farmhouse style. What has been called "a delightful walk down memory lane" unfolds at a camping-friendly fairgrounds. Two Extravaganzas (May and Sept.) draw 2,000 vendors.
springfieldantiqueshow.com

FRIENDLY EVERY WEEKEND
The Raleigh Market
**Raleigh, North Carolina,
every Saturday and Sunday**

Free admission, free parking and free to bring your pup along make this dog-friendly weekender a welcoming place to roam. Over 500 indoor-outdoor vendors offer everything from antiques, vintage clothing, furniture, jewelry and collectibles to the handcrafted, homegrown, home-baked and just plain unusual.
theraleighmarket.com

HIP HANGOUT
Brooklyn Flea
**Brooklyn, New York,
weekends year-round**

Founded in 2008, this relative newcomer transitions from indoor to outdoor in season. Both the crowds and the press rave about the furniture, vintage clothing, collectibles and antiques, as well as jewelry, art, and handmade goods by local artisans. It wouldn't be Brooklyn without great food thrown in the mix. Shop two locations: one on Saturday, one on Saturday and Sunday.
brooklynflea.com

43

CHAPTER 2

STEP INSIDE

Explore the unique decor that gives these homes their style.

Feeling Farmhouse

New homeowners embrace DIY, reclaimed materials and choice antiques for their Connecticut abode.

FOR RENT

Both the living room and loft space (opposite) feature rustic beams by AZ Faux Beams.

WELCOME HOME
"I love how bright and open the living room feels," says Kaley Cutting of her favorite room in her new house. The 20-foot ceilings add a feeling of spaciousness.

Just because a home was built in 2008, that doesn't mean it has to look or feel like it. The name of Kaley Cutting's blog, The Little White Farmhouse, is a giveaway that she's joyfully obsessed with the romantic world of farmhouse, antiques and shabby-chic decorating. Over the past few years, since she and her husband purchased their first home, she has been designing and renovating it to reflect that very style.

"I'll admit, I've always dreamed of owning an authentic farmhouse, with acres of land and a barn, so we could start our own little farm," she sighs. "But we thought it would be smarter to own a newer home, as first-time home buyers on a budget. So we have created our own DIY farmhouse by adding shiplap, installing antique brass chandeliers and beams and painting everything white."

Elements that Cutting favors—gallery walls, antiques and a foundation of neutral colors with pops of green—all come together to greet anyone who comes through the door. "My best find has to be the

HAVE A SEAT
Mismatched dining chairs pair with a pillow-lined banquette in this inviting dining nook.

This is the same DIY shiplap that Cutting and her husband made for the bedroom from 1-by-6 pine boards.

UNDER FOOT
A vintage runner from the website The Ethical Home—which carefully and ethically sources its textiles—fills a hallway off the kitchen.

CLEAN START
Classic subway tiles with gray grout was a dramatic yet budget-friendly part of the kitchen reno. The faucet ties in with the shelving brackets.

"I've always dreamed of owning an authentic farmhouse, with acres of land and a barn."

Kaley Cutting

ALWAYS READY
Cutting reserves this buffet for two of her loves: fresh morning coffee and seasonal decorating.

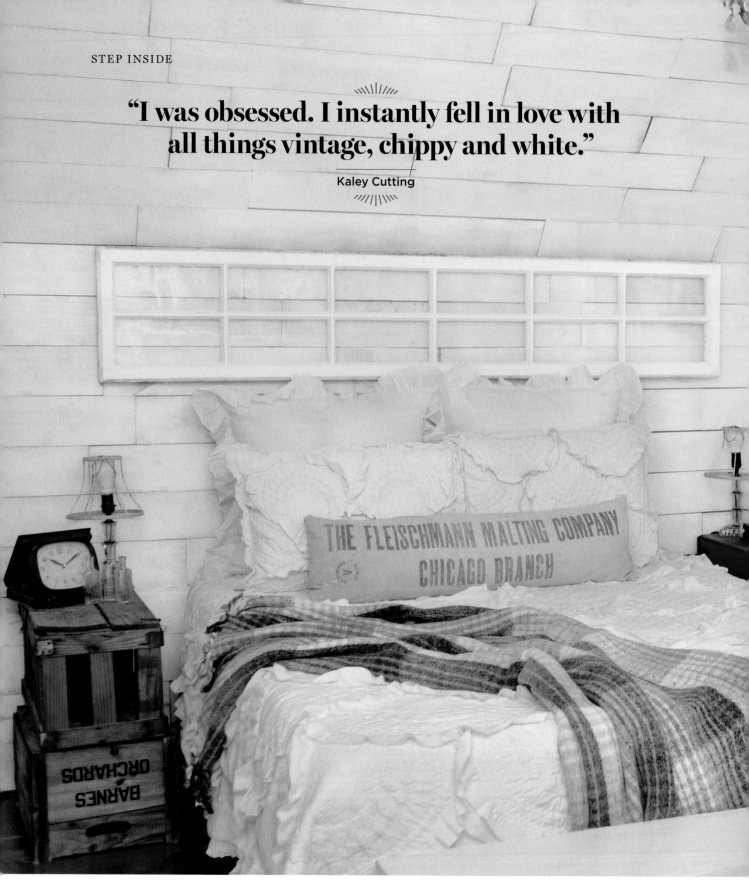

"I was obsessed. I instantly fell in love with all things vintage, chippy and white."

Kaley Cutting

THE FLEISCHMANN MALTING COMPANY
CHICAGO BRANCH

BARNES ORCHARDS

DIY DÉCOR
Cutting and her husband used 1-by-6 pine boards (some cut shorter) and white spray paint to make their own shiplap.

chippy green lockers I scored from a local antiques shop," she says. "They are such a statement piece in our entry, and that color of green is my absolute favorite."

Cutting became inspired years ago when she stumbled across Liz Marie Blog, a DIY, décor and lifestyle blog centered around one couple's Michigan farm. "Back at that time, she was living in a newer split-level that she made into her own dream farmhouse—and I was obsessed. I instantly fell in love with all things vintage, chippy and white."

Their own "farmhouse" sits on 5 private acres and won the couple over with its 20-foot cathedral ceilings, cozy loft and open-concept living, dining and kitchen space. Old signs, mirrors, fans, portrait photographs, cobblers' forms, trunks, lanterns and military relics are pieces Cutting now finds hard to resist. "My top vintage-shopping tip is to go beyond your local antiques shops," she says. "I have found some amazing pieces for a steal on Craigslist, on Facebook marketplace and at Goodwill. If there's something I'm really on the hunt for, I can always find it on Etsy." Her modern formula for a vintage look certainly has her family, friends and her Instagram followers feeling very farmhouse.

@thelittlewhitefarmhouse

53

Room-divider curtains match the $50 thrifted French sofa. Both counter the pop of a Yahyali rug from Turkey.

Turkish Delight

Eccentric pieces from across the globe mingle with family heirlooms to create a Southern home with bohemian flair.

A tall cabinet topped with plants and ceramic pieces softens a corner and brings the eye up, while adding storage.

WHEEL NICE
Diaz's dad made the living room's wagon wheel table. "It is such a special piece for me; it will always be my coffee table no matter what décor I have," she says.

Many people say every piece in their home has a story. Anita Diaz really means it: There isn't a square foot of her abode that lacks an emotional connection, right down to the land underneath. Though built in 2007, the home sits on scenic mountain property in North Carolina that has been in her family for five generations.

"My great-grandfather was one of three original settlers in Palm Beach/Dade County, Florida, and this was his summer home," Diaz shares. "There are several original buildings still on the property, along with a mountain creek I grew up playing in. So after traveling in the Air Force, it was literally coming home for me."

Diaz and her husband are musicians and U.S. Air Force veterans who settled in western North Carolina a dozen years ago to raise their children. She has always loved the creative aspects of decorating and jumped on board "when blogging really took off" about nine years ago. "I launched whisperingpineshomestead.net as a site dedicated to using what you have to make a house a home. I'm really passionate about making my home a warm, nurturing and welcoming place for my family, and I feel it's so very important to have a place where one feels safe and protected from the stress and worries of everyday life."

FAMILY TIES
A 1953 painting by Diaz's late uncle, Montana artist Rex Thrower, hangs under antlers from the first deer her father killed (for food). Diaz made the dining table from wood she salvaged on the family property. A local craftsman fabricated the base she designed.

Midcentury dining chairs make a modern juxtaposition in a room of antiques and special heirlooms.

A bench re-covered in burlap gets a seasonal update with a woven rug.

Runners top the piano and 1880s organ. Diaz made the patterned one from Turkish textiles.

Diaz covered the wall behind a German antique art print (early 1900s) in vintage sheet music.

Living in a newer home only strengthened her desire to connect with the past. She found herself fascinated with the original Victorian farmhouse her dad grew up in on the site. (The farmhouse was torn down in 1960.) As fate would have it, her grandfather had stored everything from "the old house" that was salvageable in one of the other buildings on the property: from solid wood doors, stair treads and windows to wormy chestnut trim, beadboard, tongue-and-groove boards, and other bits and pieces.

"When I found this stash of treasures, exactly as he had left it in 1960, I felt like it had been saved for me!" she shares. "So we started to incorporate everything we could into our home." Next, she searched her parents' attic, her dad's garage and even the old root cellar and smokehouse and discovered furniture, wood boxes, tables, lamps and countless other treasures that could be repurposed as décor.

Her evolving style focuses on authenticity. American style with elements of farmhouse and country blends with eclectic pieces she has inherited from across the world, along with gems she collected herself while traveling. The subtle bohemian flair that distinguishes her home emerged naturally and is ever-changing.

"I have added wrought iron, carpets and pottery I bought in Turkey and Bolivia, to a collection of Blue Willow I bought in Japan, to Native American art I have collected for years, inherited Chinese ancestor prints, and a beautiful inherited collection of brass from India and China," Diaz says. "I've fallen in love with all things 1970s lately and have been incorporating some of those colors and textures from my childhood, including a record player, Pieri lamp and macramé. I also love the authentic tribal patterns of pillow covers that are made from vintage

HARMONIOUS DESIGN
Diaz started playing piano at 3, earned a degree in music and joined the U.S. Air Force as a vocalist/pianist. Her "groovy" music room isn't just for looks. "It's a creative space, so it needs to inspire," she notes.

Open shelving is as practical as it is decorative, keeping oft-used pieces handy.

The wilder side of boho emerges in this bright floral print. Diaz swaps out the sink skirt seasonally.

kilims and have found some great deals online directly from Turkey."

In the master bedroom is a drop-leaf table her grandmother used to fold laundry on. "My dad played under it as a child, and I fold my laundry on it now. I think of her every time," she says. A radio from the 1940s belonged to her great-grandmother. "My dad remembers listening to FDR's funeral on it. The connection to that event so long ago is surreal for me."

Diaz has a knack for layering historic significance with memories made by hand. The couple fashioned kitchen countertops from wormy chestnut wood they pulled off a building on their land, replaced interior doors with five-panel wood doors from the old house, and restored an iron bed they found on the property. Her most beloved DIY is a corner cabinet her husband crafted from slabs of a walnut tree her dad cut in the 1970s. It features more wormy chestnut as trim. "For me, that piece brings everything together: the past with the present," she explains. "You cannot buy that in any store."

She always favors reusing, repurposing and recycling. From antique dinnerware to rewiring a 1970s lamp or recovering an old lampshade, Diaz augments pieces of the past with hand-sewn draperies, pillow covers and table runners.

Each colorful room captures her family's past and present. "When people scroll through Instagram, I don't want my feed to be mistaken for anyone else's. I want my home to reflect who we are, where we've been, and what is important to us. Our home has to tell our story."

> ▸ **BACK IN TIME**
> Generations of memories fill the bedroom. Her grandmother's trunk and great-grandmother's quilts join curtains Diaz's mother made in the 1970s. Diaz restored the inherited bed.

◂ **RECIPE FOR LOVE**
Vintage fills the kitchen, from a 1965 radio to Pyrex and McCoy pieces from her mother. Diaz made the macramé planter; she and her husband made the countertops from old wood.

> ⑊⑊⑊⎮⎮⎮⫽⫽⫽
> # "I really don't have a favorite room. I try to give every room something special that makes me smile when I walk in."
>
> Anita Diaz
> ⫽⫽⫽⎮⎮⎮⑊⑊⑊

This gallery wall includes a basket from Gale Nation's mom and a drawing her husband made at age 6.

PERSONAL DÉCOR
The pillows in the entry have significance: Gale Nation's husband is a proud Cheyenne, Wyoming, native; he and his dad were both Eagle Scouts.

Globe Trotter

Maps and globes are just two of this artist's beloved collections that are scattered around her home and studio. Each piece is a muse for her creativity.

A cluster of vintage metal globes always catches the eye, whether in an antique shop or a home, stirring up a bit of wanderlust for faraway places and exotic adventures.

In Gale Nation's Kansas City, Kansas, home, these globes are a common sight. Yet, like everything else in the house Nation and her husband, Vic, share, a meaningful story encircles those nostalgia-inducing orbs. "I've been collecting globes and globe banks since I was a child," says the full-time artist and business owner. "I still have the metal globe bank I got for opening a savings account, and the light-up globe I got in third grade because I wanted to find the places I was reading about." Her lifelong love of maps and globes was born before she finished grade school. "Now my entire business is based on travel-themed items with words that mean something to people. I still always buy metal globes wherever I go. I'll never have enough."

During those same formative years, a skill emerged, one she inherited from her father, who had beautiful penmanship. "I could read and write cursive before I went to first grade, so no one was sure what to do with me!" she says with a laugh. Those early inklings combined with a degree in interior design from the University of Oklahoma have shaped Nation's livelihood. Her days, and her home, are filled with art, design, hand-lettering and calligraphy.

In addition to teaching workshops, classes and retreats where she supports others in trying their hand at fanciful lettering, this born-and-bred Kansas girl is a freelance artist for Hallmark. Her products line its shelves and she also sells them close to home at the monthly West Bottoms market. Those First Friday weekends draw shoppers from across Kansas City, who relish its blend of art, vintage, makers and food trucks that spark an energy unlike any other local gathering.

Nation's line of hand-lettered maps, globes, apparel and home décor mirrors the personal collections around her home, including her lower-level studio. It was that sunny space where she initially envisioned working and teaching workshops that sealed the deal for the artist.

"I knew the minute I saw this house listed online that it was ours," she recalls. "It hadn't been touched since it was built in 1980. It was a mess, but it had great potential. When we were walking through, Vic kept telling me I was crazy—until he saw the lower garage." A four-car tandem garage on the lower level meant the couple would no longer need to carry her work supplies up and down the stairs as they had in their previous home. A two-car garage upstairs allowed them to reclaim the indoor parking spots they had relinquished for storage.

When the couple moved in three years ago, Nation set about lightening and brightening every inch. "I wanted this home to be mainly white as a background for my collections. And I like to change up colors in accessories frequently," she says. A great contractor, an extensive reno and a tight time line later, the home makes their world go 'round. If only they could have skipped all that work in progress.

The pair lived in the lower level during construction on the upper two floors, then moved to the third floor while the crew finished the lower level. "It was dusty

and we had no kitchen, but I loved every minute. My husband? Not so much!" says Nation. Before they could begin, the inside had to be painted with Kilz to remove lingering pet odors. From there, the project included addressing termite damage; tearing out three walls in the living room; pulling down yards of 1980s drapes, valances and sheers; removing carpet and tile and replacing it with hardwood floors; re-carpeting the entire upstairs; redoing all 4½ baths; and repainting the interior and exterior. "I loved seeing the progress every day and I was able to make a lot of on-the-spot decisions," she adds. "We started the remodel the day after Labor Day and our furniture was delivered the night before Thanksgiving."

Freshly painted, and with all the dust cleared, the home has fulfilled Nation's expectations as the perfect

PACKED UP
Nation's love of vintage suitcases keeps the towering stack in the corner ever-changing. Each of them also serves as storage space.

FRESH LOOKS
In front of the plate wall, a vintage peanut machine holds flowers, and the glass terrarium is home to a new themed display each month.

65

ROYAL SERIES
SOUTH AMERICA
A. J. NYSTROM & CO. CHICAGO

Pull-down
school maps
make colorful
wall-hangings for
large spaces.
No framing
required!

SPACE FOR ANOTHER
Nation always finds room to squeeze
just one more globe into the big green
cabinet in the couple's living room.

place for both work and relaxation. One of her favorite spots is the newly opened-up dining room that looks out to a pond. Who can believe it used to be a closed-in porch that served as a claustrophobic office? "There's an amazing sunset every night out there, and the water makes me feel grounded," she says. Light pours into the entire house and, with its white walls, the colorful pieces she's arranged there add a vibrant pop.

"I love a collected, vintage look that doesn't look matchy and has a sentimental feel to it—but I also hate clutter," Nation says. "I corral things with trays and baskets to group them and keep them neat. Everything in our home has a story behind it, and that's what matters to us most."

Beyond the tales behind each map and globe, Nation holds a strong connection to heirlooms she's collected from her parents' house and from her grandparents.

Her dad made her entry table in his eighth-grade shop class; the coat rack was dug out of the trash from the Wyoming State Capitol, where her mother-in-law was the real estate commissioner. She inherited her hope chest from her great-aunt, along with a rack of teacups and saucers. "I used to love to choose one and drink tea with her," Nation shares. "She and my great-grandmother also made most of my vintage quilts. The plate wall features every state we've lived in and where

FLOWER POWER
A tablecloth covers the love seat cushion in the studio. Nation used baby blue spray paint on the trunk that she scored for $5 at a garage sale.

BLUE RIBBON FOODS

WORLD VIEW
On the living room hearth, more globes gather in an old soda crate and atop small books.

our kids live now, along with family china. I only collect what I really love—but it's still a lot!"

The lower-level studio area holds four big vintage dining tables. Groups of girlfriends gather around them for wine-and-crafts nights and students take up their pens in Nation's classes. "I've held two art retreats here and there's plenty of room for everyone and our supplies. It even has a great view!" This artist with an eye for home design is also the hostess with the mostess in her reimagined vintage-filled home.

@galenation

"I wanted this home to be mainly white as a background for my collections. And I like to change up colors in accessories."

Gale Nation

Let this be the year you choose courage over fear

is the way I share my soul with the world

what a wonderful world

REMEMBER who you wanted to be

Nation's art and hand-lettered inspirational phrases fill one wall to cheer her art students on.

HAPPY PLACE
In the studio, tablecloths from Nation's grandmother drape the tables; a chenille-covered vintage chair is a favorite seat.

69

Midcentury modern looks are characterized by clean lines and mixed materials.

SOFA SO GOOD

The time-capsule living room features Gobeil's grandmother's coffee table from the 1950s. "I am obsessed with the sectional!" she says. A local collector was selling the unusual piece and asked everyone who was interested to place a blind bid. "I guess I wanted it the most because I bid everything I had saved for a couch, and I won."

Midcentury Modern

Thanks to a cohesive color scheme and collectible pieces from the 1950s and 1960s, every room captures a favorite era.

CLASSIC ROCKER
A midcentury-style
rocking chair seems to
glow with natural light
under a vintage tripod
lamp. Gobeil's choice
of furnishings with
minimal frames, legs
and bases keeps the
look light and floaty.

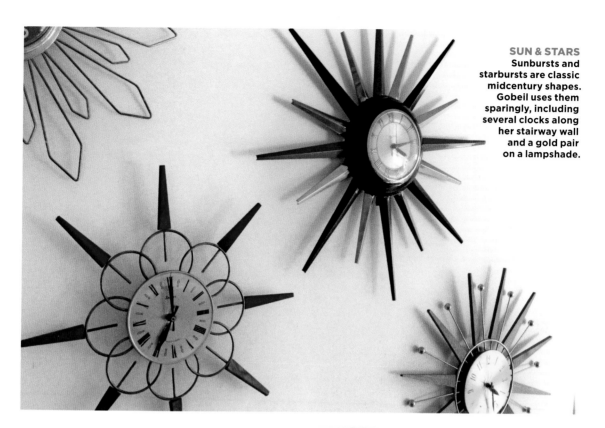

" have loved everything vintage since I was very young," says Chelsi Gobeil, who lives in a 1980s home cleverly styled to evoke a much different blast from the past. "I remember watching *Grease* in grade two. After that, there was no looking back!"

She shares her family home in Regina, Saskatchewan, Canada, with her husband, Paul; their fun-loving 3-year-old daughter, Paisley; and their little dog, Lucy. A devoted elementary school teacher, Gobeil says her dream job would have been as set designer for *Mad Men*.

"My grandma had a time-capsule house, beautifully decorated with great '50s and '60s touches, including a pink bathroom she tiled herself," she recalls. "I was fascinated by her trinkets, my mom's old bedroom, old toys in the basement and the photo albums—I loved it all." She grew up on '60s music and became a lifelong Beatles fan. (She actually got called onstage at a Paul McCartney concert, and he autographed her wrist—she had it tattooed on that very night!)

Her passions include midcentury architecture, design, music, fashion and history. "There will never be a time when things from the '50s and '60s don't make me giddy!" she exclaims.

A mix of organic elements like succulents and graphic shapes like the starburst lamp pair perfectly.

THIRD TIME'S THE CHARM
"When decorating my credenza or hi-fi, I adorn them minimally and often place items in groups of three," Gobeil says. "That way, the furniture is still the focal point and elevated to an art form in itself."

Though the home was built in 1983, Gobeil embraced its quiet location—with a backyard creek—along with its midcentury-style elements. Bountiful open space, exposed-beam ceilings, large windows, skylights and built-in shelves ticked her dream-house boxes. "I love to host parties, and this house has a huge, quirky bar in the basement, a wet bar on the main floor and a large kitchen island. It was built for entertaining!" she says. A commercial artist once lived there, and the couple opted to keep a massive mural of a landscape with hot-air balloons that covers a basement wall.

Gobeil harnessed her nostalgia for a time she never experienced to design an authentic ode to her favorite era, shaken and stirred with individuality. She has been collecting since high school, and her mod dresses are only the beginning. She groups collections smartly and keeps it simple. A few starburst clocks (like the one pictured on the opposite page) hang over the stairs. She limits vintage barware to black, gold and white to keep them cohesive.

"Midcentury modern is an amalgamation of functionality, form and style," she notes. "Think clean lines, uncluttered areas, bright and airy rooms. Less is more." Just a few months after moving in, Gobeil

IT'S HAPPY HOUR
After cleaning up a $20 barware cabinet, Gobeil painted the side panels in retro aqua. As a finishing touch, she added two starbursts, repurposed from a set of old candleholders.

BURSTING OUT
A vintage starburst clock in electric blue brightens up the wall.

FEELING BLUE
"My favorite colors are pink, turquoise and aqua, and, when decorating, my eye is always drawn to these colors," Gobeil says. Instead of choosing one, she blends both.

scored a curvy vintage sectional—and her vision started to take off.

One palette for the open-concept main floor ensures that from any angle, colors complement one another instead of competing or clashing. Minty shades of aqua, turquoise and teal, with white and teakwood, stay true to the period. "Which was easy because most of the pieces are from those decades," Gobeil adds. "The single palette also works well when introducing new décor items. I can move them from room to room, and they work in most places."

Gobeil believes timeless style defies any fad factor and bucks the advice that mixing in modern items prevents a space from looking dated. "I find that midcentury-modern pieces look fresh, despite being more than 60 years old," she says. "The fact that some are still in production says it all. Many rooms from the era have stood the test of time." And she's always on the hunt for new (old) pieces: She waits in estate-sale lines, uses the VarageSale app and goes to thrift stores weekly with a friend. "After 15 years, I still love the anticipation of finding a treasure."

 @gobeil_soleil

GOOD DAY, SUNSHINE
Feel-good vibes permeate these
two happy rooms. "The kitchen
and sunroom are so bright
and cheery," says Gobeil. The
couple painted the sunroom a
buttery yellow and converted
it into a seasonal playroom for
their daughter. Gobeil's advice?
"Marry someone who doesn't
mind when you paint interior
doors pink and who will pick up
and haul furniture home from
garage sales for you!"

Tropical Staycation

Why plan an escape when you have a cozy, colorful cottage filled with vintage finds from the Sunshine State?

EXIT HERE
Michele Mancini painted the back entrance in several colors that evoke the cottages of Key West. Through a dog door, her pups have garden access.

They say paint is the fastest, easiest, most affordable home redo. And we think this cottage proves it!

Palm-leaf prints are everywhere now, but Mancini makes her own statement by pairing them with stripes.

Vintage McCoy Pottery vases hold lush arrangements that match the design scheme.

t's hard to miss the hideaway of East Coast designer—and now full-time Florida resident—Michele Mancini. From the street, the brightly colored Sarasota, Florida, cottage peeks out from behind a picture-perfect picket fence tangled in fragrant white jasmine.

The interior is a vibrant rainbow of vintage furnishings arranged in charming retro vignettes. "I have always had a love affair with nostalgia," she says.

In fact, Mancini's passion for the past inspired her to establish a successful textile-design firm. Her exuberant fabrics catch the eye in her own house but can also be found in those of many celebrities, including Bruce Springsteen, Barbra Streisand, Bruce Willis, Bette Midler and others. Her textiles, which she describes as "modern classics with Hollywood glamour," have seduced the film industry as well, appearing in movies such as *The Mambo Kings*, *The Marrying Man* and *A River Runs Through It*, to name a few.

In spite of her success, while searching for a home away from home, the designer succumbed to the quirky allure of a then-dilapidated cottage. Today,

COME ON BACK
Shades of aqua, turquoise and green harmonize on the enclosed back porch, where shelves display a collection of vases, watering cans and sand pails. Old sofas were given a second chance with new upholstery and cushy pillows covered in Mancini's fabrics.

81

ISLAND TIME
A mix of flea market finds, unique lamps, animal prints and floral textiles give the living room its cozy tropical feel and bring to mind scenes from Havana and Hawaii.

JUICY FRUIT
Oranges are a Florida staple, whether as refreshing ingredients or pretty garnish. A vintage flag peers from under glass on this makeshift cocktail table.

83

This door has it made in the shade: a vintage glass knob, hooks for a sun hat and cover-up, and contrasting trim.

DOG-FRIENDLY DIGS
Mancini's dogs feel more than welcome in her happy abode with its focus on comfort and indoor-outdoor living. They love spending time in the garden or on the porch.

85

STEP INSIDE

this compact 1920s dwelling is a star in its own right—a lively, multihued confection with a lot more grace than space.

Never one to take herself too seriously, Mancini describes her style as eclectic, with the soul of a purist. "I do group things from the same periods by rooms," she says of her methods. The key to her successful decorating strategy lies in a well-balanced mix of imaginative arrangements, accessories, accent colors and an infusion of her own playfully patterned fabrics.

Because the cottage is so tiny, Mancini has stretched the visual space by removing the interior doors and linking adjacent rooms with a unified color scheme. Walls bathed in celadon and celery hues create a soothing repetition. Door and window frames receive a contrasting color treatment, which defines them whimsically.

To achieve a romantic mood in the dining room, Mancini painted the ceiling a deep, rich blue reminiscent of a summer night sky. Instead of predictable art, framed fabric samples from her line dress up the back wall.

The neighboring living room owes its restful and inviting feeling to warm shades of purple and green. On one wall, below a textured grass cloth ceiling hangs a collection of hand-colored old Florida photographs. Mancini made the most of the ordinary fireplace by painting its bricks an avocado green, turning the mantel into a changing stage for various collections, and using the hearth as a display spot for favorite pots and candles.

The designer's sunny outlook comes to life in the kitchen. The once-dismal cubicle is now awash in hot hues like four-alarm red, banana yellow, emerald green and Caribbean blue. The cheerful theme continues in the adjoining turquoise back porch furnished with vintage pieces from the Sunshine State, including an assortment of old metal sand pails and what she lovingly calls "garishly endearing" chalkware vases.

Small in stature yet generous in unpretentious comfort, Mancini's cottage celebrates its vibrant topical setting and her ebullient personality. Anyone who walks by its cheerful façade feels like they already know her.

JUNGLE BOOGIE
Three shades of green bring the dining room to life, while Mancini's barkcloth fabrics are a perfect fit for the Florida cottage setting, and the McCoy Pottery vases hold greenery collected from the garden.

A dual burst of orange pops through the doorway of this green room with a blue ceiling.

Talk about a gallery wall! This one sticks to a botanical theme: fabric in antique frames of similar proportion.

87

Saved by Soul

A shopper, reseller and survivor finds healing in decorating
her home with vintage loves and sharing it with the world.

Original wood ceilings meet white shiplap and big, repurposed barn doors on sliders.

HOME COMFORTS
Behind the leather couch with flour-sack pillows in the living area is a bookshelf Joe repurposed from flea market scaffolding and boards.

89

FOR THE LOVE OF IT
"I've only been on Instagram for a couple years," Contreras says. "I was doing all of this decorating with vintage for us, not an audience."

To see Dawn Contreras greet the stream of repeat customers stopping by her booth, one would guess this funky California girl had been selling at San Diego–area flea markets for decades. Her eye-catching jeans are vintage, adorned with vibrant patches of salvaged fabric coupled with swatches of beautifully preserved vintage embroidery. Floral Doc Marten boots complete her signature look. Her quirky, rustic-romantic fashion sense alone would be a reason to

stop by. But all around her, Contreras' booth is as charming, curated and one-of-a-kind as she is.

"I never thought in my wildest dreams that I would be selling at these markets," says Contreras, referring to the Coast Vintage Market in Mission Viejo and The Barn Vintage Marketplace's flea markets that pop up in Santa Ysabel three times a year. "Brandi and Cierra Smothers, a mother and daughter who own The Barn, saw something in me that I didn't see in myself. I love their antique shop and have bought the most

ON THE MOVE
In a cozy living room corner, the goodies that fill an open blue cabinet with a red interior are in constant flux. Any holiday is an excuse to redo!

An antique metal form changes by the season; for fall, it holds several sparse branches.

THE ARTS

Once you hang an old piano on the wall, you're not playing by anyone else's decorating rules!

amazing treasures there. Brandi and I hit it off, and I would bump into her at the markets. She gave me four months to gather things for my first sale. Since then, I've been figuring it out as I go."

Contreras began selling just a year-and-a-half ago with the support of her husband, Joe, and son, Alex, who actively share her passion for picking. For the past 25 years, the family has bonded by traveling up and down the West Coast in search of vintage treasures. Prized souvenirs of those trips comprise the bulk of their home's décor. Just about everything but their leather sofa is a proudly sourced vintage piece.

Contreras' jubilant evolution from shopper to sharing her home on social media to market seller was born out of a sad set of circumstances. Four years ago, as her mother suffered from Alzheimer's, she left a career in retail to help care for her, along with her sister-in-law, Candi. During her years as a caretaker, Contreras was diagnosed with breast cancer.

"Vintage saved me," she shares. "When I left my job, I got really interested and involved in it. I found it to be very therapeutic. My son set up an Instagram account for me. He thought it would be a good diversion while I was going through my treatments. Instagram has an amazing community, and it has opened so many doors."

The positive feedback she received lifted her spirits immensely. The more photos of the soulful, vintage aspects of her home that she posted, the more motivated she became to "up her game" and take her home to the next level, slowly swapping out the mix of old and new for strictly vintage and antique furnishings and décor. "I was getting a response—and that got me even more inspired," Contreras recalls.

For a while, she resold vintage clothing and knickknacks on eBay. Then Brandi invited her to become a seller. "My husband and son were my biggest cheerleaders, but she really had to convince me!" Contreras says. "I had been going to swap meets every weekend for 30 or 40 years. The last four or five years, we went whole-hog vintage on the house. But I guess my years of merchandising at Macy's also helped."

The home that inspired it all is a visual feast of various styles. "Truth be told, I love it all!" Contreras says with a laugh. "I would describe it as vintage farmhouse meets boho chic meets industrial vintage. We're very collected and have a little of everything. And that's what I sell. If it's in my booth, it's something I would decorate with. If I don't love it, I don't buy it."

For the wall treatment, they used rags to apply green paint to a white wall, then rubbed in gold, sparingly.

BRIGHT STAR
Contreras blends farmhouse primitive, industrial and vintage touches with color and whimsy. She calls this space "the green room."

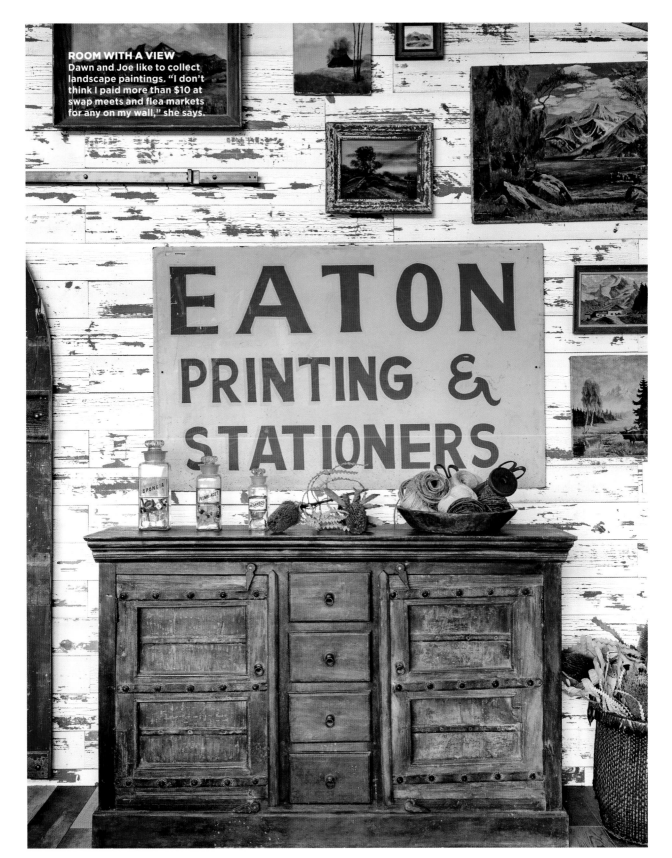

ROOM WITH A VIEW
Dawn and Joe like to collect
landscape paintings. "I don't
think I paid more than $10 at
swap meets and flea markets
for any on my wall," she says.

EATON
PRINTING &
STATIONERS

COLOR DELIGHTS Photographic cards for the antique stereoscope on top of the cabinet fill the slots below. Between the kitchen and the dining room, a tiled arch serves as a decorative pass-through; stacks of vivid Fiestaware peek through a glass cupboard door.

Built in the 1950s, the colorful abode has provided a canvas for the family's creativity for 15 years. Their contractor, Ernesto Castellanos, helped them mount a beyond-repair piano to create shelving on one wall. Joe worked his magic on scaffolding purchased at a flea market to craft a bookcase, morphed a midcentury workbench into a TV stand, built a backyard farm table and collaborated with Contreras on whimsical wall treatments throughout the home.

Apparently, good things happen when you marry the boy next door. The couple met when Dawn was 9 and Joe was 12. They began dating five years later and just celebrated their 30th wedding anniversary. Their home has evolved along with them. Most recently they remodeled the kitchen—installing blue shiplap, raising the ceiling, replacing tired appliances and adding open shelving for Fiestaware.

Now Dawn and Joe are casually on the hunt for a home that's a certified antique, at least 100 years old. "But that's down the road," she explains. In the meantime, they're toying with the idea of opening a retail shop—a permanent place for Contreras and

PERFECT SOUVENIR
Contreras loves to hang-dry herbs and flowers in the kitchen. She found the 80-year-old butcher-block island on a road trip to Lake Tahoe.

BLOCK PARTY
The Spanish Village Art Center inside San Diego's Balboa Park inspired this alfresco dining area. Joe built the farm table, which can seat eight.

Contreras found the blocks on Craigslist; the family painted them to resemble the pavers in Balboa Park.

San Diego has a number of tile houses that supply Spanish and Mexican tile.

OLD-WORLD CHARM
Joe designed the backyard tile fountain as a focal point; they had seen one similar in Old Town San Diego. Their contractor built it with a crew.

her followers. "I love everything about vintage. I love buying it, wearing it, decorating with it and selling it," she says, adding that Instagram is part of her model for success.

A woman who follows her feed drove three hours each way from Northern California to shop the booth. Contreras clicked with another woman from Kansas, so they went junking together when she happened to be in Southern California with her husband on business. Once a week, Contreras posts sneak peeks of recent finds that she plans to bring to the next market.

"The interaction is really fun. As soon as it's not fun, I wouldn't do it," Contreras says of the social media platform that enhances her vintage-infused life. "I've been able to connect with so many wonderful people" who admire her chippy interiors and the chance to meet her at the markets.

📷 *@earlydawn22*

MAKE A SPLASH
A Turkish kilim rug from eBay and a pair of Urban Outfitters blue chairs provide a burst of color amid neutral finds from estate sales and vintage shops.

Made by the artist homeowner: the front door's wreath, yarn tassels and the floral vanity/desk.

Signature Style

Estate sale finds and hand-painted furniture took this artist's house from plain-Jane to packed-with-personality.

n the Overland Park suburb of Kansas City, Missouri, Nicole Mertz makes a signature mark just about everywhere she goes. From her lilac-dusted curls to her chartreuse front door that she painted to match a favorite purse, this "Jack of all trades artist," interior stylist and floral designer seems to naturally leave a rainbow of good vibes in her wake.

Up until recently, she also owned a booth in the historic West Bottoms, where she sold all the vintage treasures she scored at local estate sales. (The ones she didn't hold onto for her own home, that is.) She enjoyed the artistic side of staging the merchandise and loved meeting people from all walks of life who appreciated her rather "random" assortment of old relics and the history behind them. The booth is also where she adopted her "if you don't like something, cover it up with paint" philosophy. That credo took on a life of its own as another successful endeavor.

"I started experimenting with the broken and busted pieces I had lying around, along with less-desirable pieces from the 1970s and '80s that no one wanted," explains Mertz, who has since blossomed into a bona fide furniture artist. "I try to honor vintage, so I don't paint something I can tell doesn't want to be touched. You can tell when a piece wants to be painted. There's just something about it."

When this furniture whisperer and her husband, Josh Wright, began house-hunting in 2009, Mertz never imagined that a basic split-level house could spark such intense personal creativity and draw virtual admirers from far-flung countries on social media. But for the past decade, their 1959 abode has willingly served as an ever-changing canvas and, in recent years, an Instagrammable portfolio for Mertz's uncontained talents.

"This was not my dream house," she emphasizes. "But the midcentury homes I loved were out of our price range, and this hit all of our other criteria. It was a blank slate that allowed me to have a creative vision." Ten years in, there's no place like home for this Kansas girl.

SEEING A PATTERN
Stella the pug is patient with Mertz's propensity to change the rooms around at will. In the entry, leaded-glass windows from a thrift store stand tall on a vintage buffet that Mertz decoupaged using paper from Rifle Paper Co.

GREEN THUMB "Gardens and plants run in my family," Mertz says. "There is a tranquility to nurturing a plant and watching it grow."

Herbs aren't the only plants that have a place in the kitchen: Snake plant is a natural air purifier.

LASTING BEAUTY "When you invest in vintage, you get timeless pieces," Mertz notes. She found the green farmhouse cabinet at West Bottoms in Kansas City.

The technique Mertz used to paint this wall mimics her hand-painted ombré cabinet (at right).

One peek around her family's home quickly confirms the reason she can't choose a favorite room. A lime-green farmhouse cabinet teems with vintage pottery against a sprightly teal wall in the eat-in kitchen. Two huge pocket doors purchased at an estate sale come together to form a jaw-dropping headboard in the guest room, while leafy palm wallpaper makes a tropical statement in the master. A dainty, decoupaged floral desk that her IG followers love, a pair of recovered chairs that belonged to Josh's grandparents,

and a china hutch and Lane coffee table Mertz purchased on layaway as a 19-year-old waitress are among the pieces with memorable stories behind them.

As Nicole and Josh both work from home, spare bedrooms function as his-and-hers offices. Her hot-pink retreat complements the seasonal blooms on a tulip tree outside the window. An antique drafting table, Victorian velvet couch, batik textiles, and one of her painted furniture pieces that instills the most pride—a gigantic ombré wardrobe filled with art

"This was not my dream house. It was a blank slate that allowed me to have a creative vision."

Nicole Mertz

WORK AT HOME
Textiles create a cozy office, from the 1960s Iranian horse blanket on the wall to the vintage rugs, kilim pillows and turn-of-the-century couch that Mertz didn't sell at her booth (so she kept it).

BACK STORY
Once a backdrop in her booth, these repurposed shutters from Habitat for Humanity ReStore add texture to the dining area.

105

A quartet of floral paintings is the happy result of an online painting class by Amanda Evanston.

supplies—cozy up the space. Down the hall, Josh's office features a leather club chair surrounded by metal bookshelves, a big, old map of the city and a wooden pallet wall.

Always layered and jubilant, Mertz's imaginative surroundings marry saturated hues and confident patterns with a mélange of furnishings that include the clean, midcentury lines she favors in every room in the house. Her home is vibrant proof that color can indeed be comfortable.

"This is hard to believe now, but at first I went through and painted everything white," she says. "I needed that blank slate to see what I wanted to do with it." Next, the couple redid the hardwood floors, expanded the master suite and updated the kitchen. From there, the home's design evolution began rolling down its endless track.

"People come in and say, 'How did you do all this?'" relates Mertz. "I have to remind them that this represents 10 years of collecting and owning a vintage booth. It's been a journey. Even now, there are some parts of the house that will stay for a while—then, all of a sudden, I'll have a decorating bug hit me, or I'll want to change something, paint something or swap something out. This eclectic look doesn't happen in a week! It takes time."

Time to make decisions, time to let it all sink in—and time spent scouring estate sales. Mertz has been known to drive 90 minutes each way to an especially promising sale, often in the cold darkness before dawn. "If you want something really bad, you get there an hour or two early, put a marker down to hold your place in line, then wait in your car until it starts," she says. In an area short on flea markets, the estate sales of eastern Kansas are a must for vintage retailers and serious collectors, who queue up by 5:30 or 6 a.m. Once inside, the woman known to many as @kansasgirlvintage says she knows exactly where she is going to go, based on scanning the presale photos. She grabs what she came for, then makes another pass to dig for unexpected gems.

Initially, her grandmother turned her on to the sales. As a young child, however, Mertz had a hard time getting over the weirdness of shopping in someone else's house. Nowadays, although it still

BOARDED UP
Mounted on a pair of double
doors that belonged to the
costume designer for a local
theater is an original vintage
oil painting flanked by smaller
artworks of floral bouquets.

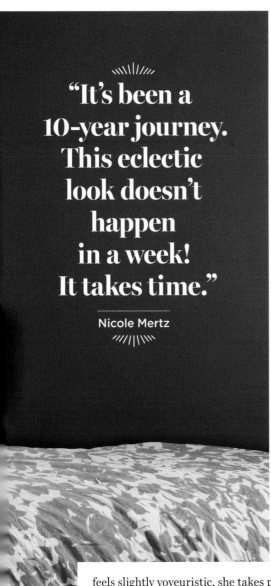

> ### "It's been a 10-year journey. This eclectic look doesn't happen in a week! It takes time."
>
> Nicole Mertz

feels slightly voyeuristic, she takes pleasure in each home's architecture, and in imagining the lives and personalities of the former occupants.

The insatiable thrill of the hunt inspires her best advice: Buy an item because you love it, and you will find the right place for it eventually. "People say, 'It's not my style,' or 'It's not my color.' I say, 'Yes, but you love it. It speaks to you. And that's enough.'"

Mertz is now taking a breather from the sometimes-cutthroat life of a vintage-booth merchant. But those early-morning estate sales—where she has unearthed countless treasures to resell—still call her by name. "It's totally an addiction," she says with a laugh. "I think that's why most people become vendors. They

have to do something with all their stuff!"

Relinquishing her booth for the time being has freed up Mertz to focus on her painting, interior styling and her work with flowers—from wreaths and floral crowns to large installations, including arbors. While unplanned events and circumstances kept Mertz from attending art school, the many avenues she has colorfully pursued are a result of her own fearless, hands-on education. "It all flows together; it's all a creative outlet," says this artist, who approaches each day with signature style. "I'm happy my life went down the creative path."

🄾 *@kansasgirlvintage*

Paint Works Wonders

Hand-painted furniture makeovers form a solid foundation for this talented Canadian's home and business.

WOOD YOU, COULD YOU?
Mary Vitullo didn't think twice about nailing pinewood boards to the wall in her airy white entryway.

On this carved Indian armoire, Vitullo used Raw Silk, one of her favorite colors by Homestead House Paint Co.

111

One visit to Mary Vitullo's blog, with its curious name, shows that she sees the world a little differently and finds endless ways to beautify it—starting with a skillful coat of paint.

Orphanswithmakeup.com is where Vitullo blogs about her adventures in repurposing vintage and antique furniture. "My furniture and thrifted finds are my little 'orphans' and my paint is the 'makeup,'" says this visionary artist based in Saint-Hubert, Quebec, Canada. "I have always been passionate about home décor and can never seem to quench my thirst for it." Since early 2013, the blog has offered an outlet for at least attempting to do so. It's also a place where she can share her finished pieces, styled in their best light and available for sale locally.

▲ LET'S PRANCE
Dreamy blues are a signature shade that appear throughout Vitullo's home, keeping it consistent. The softness of this simple stool painted in Inglenook, by Fusion Mineral Paint, is eye-pleasing under a chippy table. She also created the wood horse art.

▶ BUCKET LIST
Whether styling her furniture for photos or her home, Vitullo has a natural eye. Beside the bed (in Little Whale by Fusion Mineral Paint), floral arrangements in different sizes and shapes fill galvanized buckets. A plant rests atop a stack of books.

BEACH BABE
As pretty as
a mermaid, this
bedroom dresser
on casters wears
Ocean Breeze by
Country Chic Paint
as "makeup."

OPEN DOOR POLICY
This farm-fresh look is thanks to Homestead House Milk Paint in Sturbridge White. Vitullo added bonding agent to limit chipping.

Her builder-grade home, built in 1996, serves as both her workshop and a backdrop for photographing new pieces before she lists them on her website. "Sometimes what was to be a project ends up staying in my home," she confesses, mentioning the ombré armoire she recently reimagined with the help of four different shades of turquoise from Fusion Mineral Paint. (The step-by-step instructions are on her blog.)

"To me, vintage décor is all about filling your home with charm and character," she says. The piece joins a romantic carved sideboard she painted with milk paint and distressed, and a china cabinet in the dining room that was an heirloom from her in-laws. "We were able to make it work with our décor by giving it a fresh coat of white paint and adding barnwood to the interior backing. It gives it a whole new fresh look, one that is not as stuffy as its original dark-stained wood."

When scouting for vintage pieces she can transform, Vitullo looks for solid wood furniture with carved details she usually paints white, blue or gray. "I love so many styles, and that is definitely reflected in my home," she says. "It is a mixture of shabby chic and French country, while the kitchen is modern with vintage touches. The recent entryway refresh is sort of going in the direction of Scandinavian. I love anything with a patina."

Beyond showcasing her "orphans with makeup," the home has moved beyond its original builder-grade features thanks to Vitullo's cost-conscious personal touch. "As much as we would have preferred a fixer-upper, the thought of unknown additional expenses on an old home kind of scared us, so we opted for a new build," she says. Its proximity to a park plus great schools and services, easy access to Montreal and four bedrooms on the main floor made a strong case for working with its standard elements to create a place that felt like home.

By adding wainscoting and molding to the bedroom walls, restyling the flat, rust-colored melamine kitchen cabinets into white Shaker-style cabinets (some with glass doors), reframing windows with thicker molding, upgrading light fixtures and fashioning a kitchen backsplash from wood plank flooring and a metal table top, the couple customized their home like none other on the block.

The space proves inspiration for Vitullo's work with vintage furniture, and makes an inviting home base for her thrifting excursions. "Shop anywhere and everywhere: estate auctions, thrift stores, Craigslist, yard sales, etc.," she advises. "Find beauty in old, worn, tattered items, pieces that have beauty in their imperfections. Use odd items for displaying flowers and stack old books to decorate, possibly wrapped in twine or burlap. The key is to minimize all the other distractions, so those beautiful vintage items stand out"—with or without any painted makeup.

 @orphanswithmakeup

JUST DUCKY
The hue Duck Egg, by Annie Sloan Chalk Paint, transformed this dining table Vitullo worked on for a client who originally envisioned white.

Steal these clever ideas: Use wood flooring as wall covering and a repurposed IKEA metal tabletop as a backsplash.

COTTAGE VIBES
The centerpiece of Vitullo's kitchen is her cottage-style table and chairs. "Cottage style is laid-back, cheerful, welcoming and embraces imperfections," she says. Her sweet antique set feels romantic in Limestone from Homestead House. To make the tabletop stand out, she sanded it after one thin coat.

For added charm, Vitullo removed the fretwork from the doors and replaced the glass with wire netting.

WRITE ON
This mahogany secretary desk with a pretty crown was a dark wood that felt heavy and dated. Vitullo used two shades of milk paint, plus pink to accent its shelf.

Hang your hats as a sign of welcome, as well as a reminder to grab one for shade on your way out.

DRESS HER UP
A vintage dresser solves entry messes in style. Vitullo used Homestead House Milk Paint in Coal Black on the dresser and mirror.

COME TOGETHER
Vitullo's home has a large entryway, in which she chose to leave one wall white and plank the other with wood (opposite page). A flat rug creates just a border from the original tile and brings both sides together.

Frame black-and-white travel photos. Vitullo snapped this wild horse in North Carolina's Outer Banks.

119

Salvaged wood and a trio of oversize corbels were used to create this handmade kitchen island.

What's in Store

Canadian collectors create a cozy apartment above their downtown shop so they can stay close to their beloved antiques and handmade furniture.

Paul LeClair and Gillian Mitchell's home, which sits above their shop, Pine Sampler Furniture in Hensall, Ontario, is a fascinating display of the couple's passion and skill. One would expect the owners of a furniture and design shop to have good taste, but what this couple has done with their home goes above and beyond a good eye for vintage finds and style. Between LeClair's furniture building and woodworking and Mitchell's crafting and making, the duo have realized a unified, down-home vision for their thoughtfully renovated abode.

Muted tones, distressed furniture and quirky vintage finds fill each room. "I want it weathered, loved and lived-in," Mitchell says of what she likes to see both in their shop and in their living spaces. "We found a lovely wooden bench, but I hated the bright blue it had been painted. So I put it outside in the elements for a year—that sorted it out! The paint stripped off naturally."

OPEN UP
Behind the island, a towering pantry was made by the couple from a pair of antique doors. Mitchell's son built the timber post-and-beam room divider.

The building that houses their apartment and store dates to 1889. Since the pair moved in, it has undergone a substantial refurbishment, including a two-story addition that included a bedroom upstairs, as well as some much-needed space on the ground floor behind the shop, which is currently dedicated to LeClair's workshop.

They kicked off the remodel by stripping paneling off the walls on both floors. In the shop, they were thrilled to find rustic brick walls hidden underneath. Their excitement intensified when they discovered a lath wall under the plaster upstairs.

The original wall, covered in narrow strips of wood, adds to the feeling of stepping inside an old country home, which is enhanced by the couple's love for simple antiques and primitive furnishings.

LeClair and Mitchell don't confine the use of their skills to items for sale in their popular shop. Their home is an extension of what moves them: reimagining furniture, reinventing old objects and upcycling salvaged architectural finds. Often, LeClair does the building and Mitchell does the painting. Together, the transformed creations and the spaces they occupy feel both handmade and historic—and most of them are.

121

Although the general color palette throughout the home is subdued, there is nothing dull about this apartment. High ceilings add a lofty feeling that allows the natural light to penetrate deeper into the rooms. Well-placed painted pieces make a statement against the refinished pine floors. Against one wall, a tiny bench nearly overflows with Mitchell's endearing collection of antique teddy bears.

Even the stove is 80-plus years old, which can present the occasional challenge. "It's not simple to cook with," she admits. "But, like everything, if you give it time and watch over it properly, it works out in the end." Pots and pans hang in a cluster above the hand-built island in an open kitchen that also features a 1950s-style white fridge.

The couple isn't afraid to reproduce a vintage piece if they can't find an appropriate original. LeClair hand-paints many signs that hang on their walls; his craftsmanship makes it almost impossible to guess which is a real vintage article and which is his

▲ **SHOP SMALL**
The couple's Hensall, Ontario, store occupies an antique building. Upstairs, they built a loft living space that reflects their quirky shop.

◀ **NEW LIFE**
This large, wicker-covered glass jug (called a demijohn or carboy) would once have been used to transport or ferment wine. Now it makes a textural vase for branches.

REACHING OUT
In the living room, wooden shutters pick up the lines of the lath wall. An old apple-orchard ladder gets used for household chores.

This couple knows how to use a small corner for storage and make it look appealing!

This hefty antique pine armoire was built into a wall of their former home that dates to 1867.

SIMPLE PLEASURES
Mennonite children's clothing adds a cozy sweetness to a bedroom reading nook.

handiwork. Among other items on display are dress forms and cobblers' shoes, refurbished antique weather vanes, Mitchell's vintage-inspired handmade pillows and decorative horses the pair fashion by hand.

In the master bedroom, Mitchell boldly reworked her mother's old armchair. "I actually pulled some straw stuffing through holes I made, then removed the covers and some upholstery to reveal the basic wood and 'workings,'" she says. "I love it now!" The finishing touch is the rock-clad feature wall LeClair built by layering flat-backed stones on plywood as part of the bedroom addition.

The stone wall in the bedroom addition is simply flat-backed stones attached to plywood.

Not every couple would opt to hang vintage farm tools in the master bedroom, but it works!

GOT THE BLUES
Past a sliding barn door, blue French-style linens tie into the headboard LeClair crafted from an architectural peak and two columns.

A stack of vintage suitcases can serve as a makeshift dresser for extra blankets or off-season clothing.

EASY BREEZY
French doors let light and fresh air into the bedroom, which charms with thick wood beams and an antique dress form.

ON HIGH
Mitchell made a shelf for the bathroom from an old board supported by antique corbels. LeClair drew the dress form in charcoal to match the theme.

FANCY GOODS.

The couple has carried the narrow beadboard high on the walls to accentuate the high ceiling.

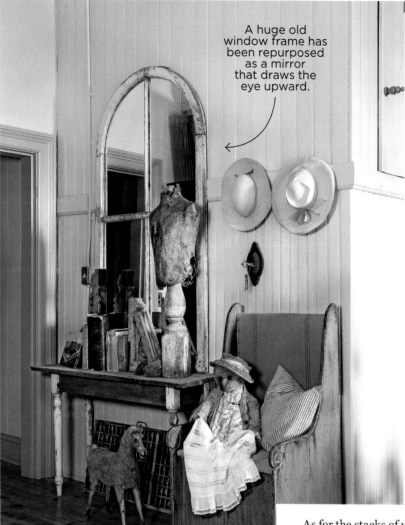

A huge old window frame has been repurposed as a mirror that draws the eye upward.

▲ **CUDDLED UP**
Antique teddy bears have a place in Mitchell's heart and in her home. Rather than display all of them together, the couple favors scattered groupings.

◄ **ALL IN THE FAMILY**
Mitchell passed her talents on to her son, Alex Oke, who handmade the large blue wooden chair as a teen. The layered entry display is collected and casual.

As for the stacks of vintage suitcases around the home, they are not mere decoration. "Everything is full!" declares Mitchell proudly. "All my crafting tools and items are in those cases." Vintage hatboxes are another place to stash supplies, while an orchard ladder in one corner of the living room is as handsome as it is functional. LeClair pulls it out whenever he needs to hang artwork or change a light bulb.

It seems fitting that the home of two shopkeepers, artisans and collectors with a deep appreciation for items from centuries past would embody a quote from 19th-century British textile designer William Morris, who once advised, "Have nothing in your houses that you do not know to be useful or believe to be beautiful." It's timelessly stylish advice.

f **@Pinesamplerfurniture**

> ## "To give people pleasure in the things they must perforce use, that is one great office of decoration."
>
> William Morris, textile designer

ROOM TO SPARE
Old hatboxes and a vintage trunk under the desk are hiding places for Mitchell's crafting supplies. A few hats and a girl's dress add whimsy.

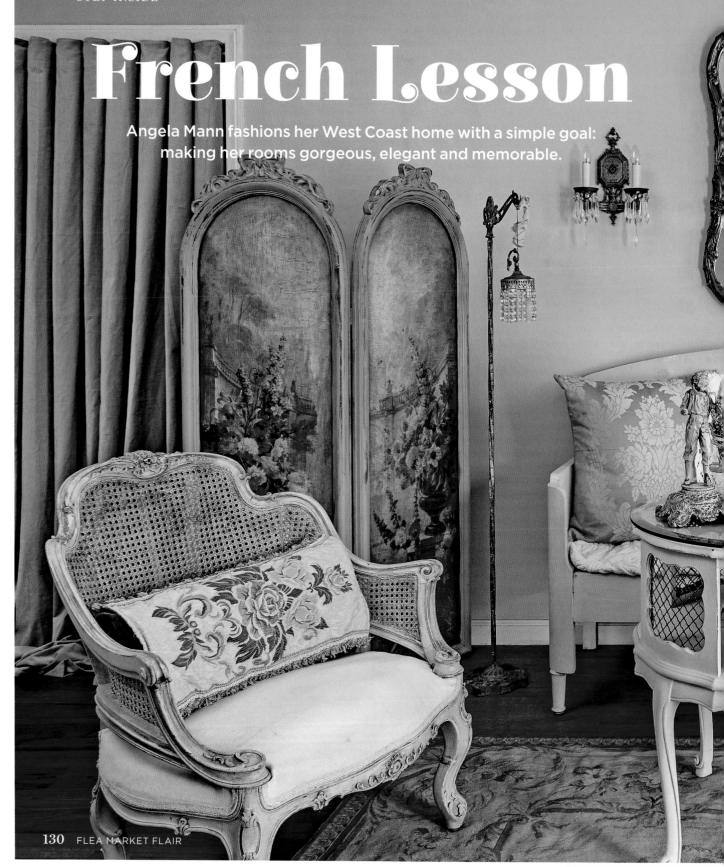

French Lesson

Angela Mann fashions her West Coast home with a simple goal: making her rooms gorgeous, elegant and memorable.

REFINED TASTES
Shapely French-style pieces speak an elegant language in the living room. A vintage screen complements pillows sewn from vintage fabric.

131

There is a lovely sense of refinement in Angela Mann's Los Angeles home, where French-style furniture is softened with fine fabrics and rooms are accented with a few select, thoughtfully arranged collections. Perhaps it's because she's had time to fine-tune her style—she's been collecting since the age of 16. "My friends wanted to go off and do silly things," she says, "and I just wanted to go to the thrift stores. They thought it was pretty weird."

Mann's love of design and vintage led her to study textiles and fashion in the 1980s and eventually to open up a bridal shop, where for years she created everything from dresses to bouquets. Now, she focuses on designing and dressing her sweet, 700-square-foot home with pretty fabrics and finds she uncovers during weekly forays to area flea markets and thrift stores.

She's the one combing through bins and baskets looking for buried treasure—like the Fortuny damask remnant she sewed into sofa pillows, or the antique French chandelier with faceted blue crystals crowning her breakfast nook.

Her corner eating area exemplifies this homeowner's talent for squeezing charm into limited square footage. The plaster urn that offers itself up as a clever table base lived in her mother's garden for years until

Dramatic window dressings give any room character. Hang sheers high and let them puddle.

◀ **PERFECT SET**
Mann is drawn to delicate lines for much of the lighting and furniture she chooses. Though she likes to say that nothing matches, the exception is clearly her beloved aqua glass vases.

▼ **WINNING LOOK**
Dried roses and hydrangea form a Victorian-infused centerpiece when tucked inside an aged trophy on a pedestal. A few fallen petals add authenticity.

Mann invited it inside and topped it with beveled glass. Hanging above, a showstopping antique French chandelier works with the glass tabletop to add some dazzle into this niche made for two. A chance find, she unearthed the lighting fixture from a box at a garage sale. Mann rewired it, then added crystals in her favorite hue: ocean blue. It complements her mermaid-worthy collection of sea-blue glassware of all vintages.

Nearby, several such pieces join a gilded mirror and flower arrangement atop a vintage cabinet with a painted rose garland. Hints of her days creating romantic bridal gowns and floral designs pop up throughout her petite jewel box of a home.

133

"Nothing stays in one place for long, and absolutely nothing matches in my house."

Angela Mann

Many of her vintage finds require some polish and repair; others might be reimagined into something else. But that's no problem. If Mann can't fix it, her father is there to help. He handcrafted the art deco–like settee in her living room from the headboard and footboard of a vintage bed. "He takes one thing and turns it into something else," Mann says. "I dream it, we discuss it, and I come back to the shop and there it is."

Luxe fabrics and curvy French-style furniture lend verve throughout the living room. Used as a portiere to mask a dark hallway, aqua velvet curtain panels create visual intrigue. A small crystal pendant is a twinkly chairside companion when suspended on a birdcage stand. And Mann rescued the three-panel floor screen, assured of its potential for beautiful functionality. She removed a damaged section and freshened the frame with paint. The piece definitely earns its keep. "I move it around and hide things behind it when people are coming over," she says.

Tucked into a sunny corner by the windows, the vintage armoire, with glass-pane doors, provides an

▲ **BOTANICAL BLISS**
For Mann, a home isn't a home without flowers. Fresh and dried blooms tie into floral prints on bed linens and porcelain.

◄ **PICTURE PERFECT**
A tall cupboard, with a curved pediment and paned glass doors, commands attention when filled with pretty dishes.

IN A NEW LIGHT
As only a French beauty can, this chandelier adds the finishing touch to the eating area. Vintage fixtures are more beguiling than new—and so is the light they cast.

Any chandelier, new or vintage, appreciates a punch of color from crystals you can add yourself.

135

GOLDEN HOUR

Bold gilt frames add visual oomph to a simple room. The two stacked here (one a portrait, one a scene) are all that were needed for "wow."

A bit of fabric, carved trim and an ornate sconce create a mini canopy over the bed like a crown.

OLD FRIENDS
Juxtaposing the richness of gilded gold with the rough texture of a vintage dress form in a complementary hue feels fresh and unexpected.

Once a Hollywood prop, this 1950s dress form has found a new calling as a jewelry model.

J.R
BAUMA
NORMAL MO
YORK, IN
N.Y.

Your best chair can't live outside, but bringing her into the garden for the day is utterly fanciful.

▲ **AN AL FRESCO AFFAIR**
Colorful collections of china and etched pink goblets make guests feel welcome.

ever-changing stage for Mann's ongoing finds. "Nothing stays in one place for long, and absolutely nothing matches in my house," Mann says of the one-of-a-kind items she discovers on her regular flea market forays.

When Mann isn't shopping for pieces and hunting down items she can repurpose into projects, she's selling them at Country Roads Antiques in Orange, California—a new strategy for refining her rooms. "My house is full of things I buy for the store then can't part with," she shares.

In the bedroom, a shapely curio cabinet is home to part of Mann's collection of treasured baubles. Others are on display across the room on a diminutive dress

form. Mann purchased it from a 90-year-old woman who designed costumes for Hollywood in the 1950s. It was likely used as a prop. Now it's the perfect size for holding her prized vintage jewelry.

She thinks standard nightstands are a snooze, so Mann opts for small tables instead. The bedside chair is made of wrought iron and likely was a garden chair before it was given a gold finish and a tufted, red velvet seat. "I love eclectic chairs," she says. "I'm basically a chair hoarder. To me, it's more interesting if they don't match."

 *@french_lilac_*

"I love eclectic chairs. I'm basically a chair hoarder. To me, it's more interesting if they don't match."

Angela Mann

Pull a bench up to your table to emphasize that romantic, mismatched look.

PARTY ON
Mann's flair for entertaining on a small scale can spread its wings outside. The lawn gives her more space to curate an inviting spread for her guests.

139

THROWBACK STYLE
Jenasie Earl's patterned 1970s couch is both comfortable and spirited. She doesn't follow the rules and loves to go bold.

Find & Seek

Attracted to a range of eras and styles, this designer and reseller creates textural spaces around gems she sources.

THE PLUSH LIFE
The sunny sunken living room features Earl's prized pair of blue velvet couches from an estate sale. She shuns window coverings here to let in light.

"First I found the living room's vintage Persian rug with jewel tones, then I went on the hunt to fulfill that color scheme."

— Jenasie Earl

"There's nothing that haunts us more than the vintage we didn't buy," says Salt Lake City interior designer and treasure peddler Jenasie Earl. With the cultivated wisdom of an old soul, Earl makes it a point to not let any compelling piece of history she spies become the one that got away.

Maybe that's why her home's luxe and layered environments are in a constant, mesmerizing state of evolution. "When I find something new, I switch out what was there and I revamp the space," she shares. "My style is very eclectic, glam and vintage. I can't pick a favorite era, so I mix them all. When you find a funky '70s couch, you just buy it and make it work!"

Earl may wear youthful teal streaks in her hair and a cheeky "Thanks, It's Vintage" T-shirt of her own design, but this thrifty 30-something mother of three has honed a mature aesthetic that gravitates toward Old World, European design—with an edge.

"My tastes and design style really make me want a home from every era," Earl says with a laugh. "The architecture of our 1975 split-level house is what I dreamed of three years ago when we moved in,

but now my heart is really starting to dream of a Victorian home with a grand, wood staircase, built-ins and original molding." Such is the burden of great taste, it seems!

Being smack-dab in the middle of remodeling her family's home one room at a time—"using as much vintage as possible"—doesn't stop Earl from sharing a stream of ongoing DIYs she completes with her husband, Chris, on her msviciousdesign.com blog and on Instagram. The vintage décor and furniture she resells locally at the Salt & Honey Market pop-up are featured in her Instagram stories.

"I feel strongly about the fact you can have a beautiful, interesting home without having to buy new," Earl affirms. "I'd say 95 percent of my home is vintage or secondhand. I use bold colors, funky wallpaper, a ton of texture and, of course, all the magical vintage pieces I can't bear to let go of. Bringing in pieces that speak to me, no matter their style and era, is what makes a personal and unique space."

She and her husband chose the home as a bigger, better fit for their growing family—and it certainly lives large. Giant windows flank the black brick

WONDER WALL The dining room's paint technique incorporates a light touch of gold leaf to frame the shelves.

Earl cherishes this hanging light that belonged to her husband's grandmother.

Floral prints in art and textiles are both retro and timeless. Pieces atop the curio cabinet with tassel handles showcase Earl's eye for the exotic.

ART LESSON
"Add depth to a wall collage by layering frames and creating a unique shape instead of a perfect square or rectangle," Earl says.

Persistence is a collector's best attribute. Earl amassed this art for less than $100 at estate sales.

"I use bold colors, funky wallpaper, a ton of texture and, of course, all the magical vintage pieces I can't bear to let go of."

Jenasie Earl

fireplace in the formal sunken living room. Nearly touching the vaulted ceiling, they bathe the space with natural light and provide curtain-free views into the backyard. Its sunny setting has made it Earl's favorite room—and her towering houseplants agree.

All those leafy, reaching and trailing specimens are just one example: Earl doesn't shy away from size or substance. Huge rugs, lanky brass candlesticks, a massive oil painting and a brawny brass shelving unit are among her finds. But they don't flutter her heart quite as much as the 8-foot-long midcentury credenza from Sweden (she swooped in and picked it up at an auction for just $70) and the boxy pair of blue velvet couches.

"I saw them in photos for an estate sale," Earl recalls fondly of the set. "I thought I was heading there early only to realize I was an hour late." Though both of the $50 couches remained when she arrived, she bought only one. "When I called my husband, he asked why I didn't buy both. But by the time I realized I needed both of them in my life, the sale had already closed." Earl says she sweated it out overnight, hoping the second was still available. Early to the sale the next morning, she couldn't believe her eyes. Not only was the second couch still there, but it was marked half off, making the pair hers for a mere $75.

"I mostly design spaces by what I find sourcing," Earl explains. "First I found the living room's vintage Persian rug with jewel tones, then I went on the hunt to fulfill that color scheme. It took me a year

BOYISH CHARM
Earl pictured an "Old English room" for her son's bedroom, and took paint darker on the trim.

SOMETHING WILD
Leopard wallpaper
from Divine Savages
provides a modern
spin on Earl's classic
Old English design.

147

ADDING DEPTH
Earl believes wallpaper offers the best
bang for your buck. The Menlo Park
pulls are by Schaub and Company;
the sconces are by Illuminate Vintage.

to find those royal blue couches, and the rest showed up throughout the process."

For her son's room, Earl discovered an antique carved-wood twin bed, which spurred the "Victorian-meets-modern" feel. "I never know how a space will turn out," she says. "I love to let the room come together organically by the pieces I find along the way."

Yet the best part about vintage, Earl adds, is the story that accompanies each piece—like the antique sewing table that serves as her nightstand. "The history of the piece had been written on the backs of the drawers," she shares. "I plan to add my own history to it."

Earl hopes she is encouraging her 23,000-plus Instagram followers that they can curate beauty on a budget—provided they are "willing to search hard for those secondhand pieces." The proof: Her entire living room cost under $1,000 and it's the room from which she derives the most satisfaction.

"Don't wait to decorate," she effuses. "Don't wait until your kids are older to have pretty vintage pieces. Your surroundings affect your mood and you deserve to have a space that creates joy. You will be happier in a space you love. And you deserve to have it now."

@msviciousdesign

BATHING BEAUTY
You don't need palatial square footage to have a soaking tub. Earl completed her retreat for the One Room Challenge without taking on a full bathroom redo.

Drama Mama

A writer's dream for her dark, mysterious
Victorian seafront home pairs shadowy paint colors
with glamorous touches for a theatrical affect.

VICTORIAN SPLENDOR
Two gray velvet Chesterfield
sofas anchor the living room,
which fronts the sea.
The walls and ceiling wear
a cocoon of Railings by
Farrow & Ball.

GOLD STANDARD
Bell uses a trick throughout her home: "Pull together a random collection of artwork by spray-painting mismatched frames gold." The purple hue in the entry hall is Pelt by Farrow & Ball.

As you walk through the plum-colored front door of the Bell home, you feel as if you are stepping into an opulent Old-World theater. The dramatic backdrop that "stay-at-home mum" and writer Peggy Bell has created is constantly changing. Just as scenery shifts during each act of a play, Bell's home alters around one cohesive narrative theme. Fresh vignettes are created frequently with thrift shop finds and newfound artwork, all while the radical changes Bell loves to experiment with are taking shape behind the scenes.

"To me, interior design is the most glorious kind of play," Bell explains. She and her husband, Phil, were very fortunate that the previous owners of their five-bedroom home overlooking a bay in Northern Ireland had completed all the necessary structural work and that the layout perfectly suited their young family of four. Bell has made it her set and her stage, indulging her creativity and her need for self-expression.

"Houses speak to me, and this one is so different from our last one," which was quite modern and minimal, she says. Keen to respond to each property individually, Bell felt strongly that this house, with its abundance of Edwardian period features, called for a very different approach. "I am a firm believer in aesthetics over function," she asserts, acknowledging a complete reversal from the modern and minimal schools of design thought, which emphasize function over decoration.

Bell's ambition to turn her home into a "Victorian gentleman's opium den" has been largely achieved. Dark walls, wingback chairs, cloistered nooks and lavish islands of elegantly displayed curios all add up to an environment where both Oscar Wilde and Sherlock Holmes would have comfortably made themselves at home. "I love floral patterns on a dark background, William Morris, anything Arts and Crafts," shares Bell. She describes her style as "boho Gothic" and says that even though she is a very selective shopper, she rarely buys anything new.

"Everything was white in here when we first moved in—so not me!" she says. "I started by painting the chimney in Pitch Black by Farrow & Ball. I loved it and just kept going."

> "I keep valuable items out of the kids' reach for sure, but honestly, most of the furniture is upcycled out of junk shops."
>
> Peggy Bell

WELCOME TO THE NEIGHBORHOOD
The house's spearmint exterior and deep-plum front door hint at the dramatic and color-conscious interior.

BLACK MAGIC
Few pieces are more theatrical
than a piano. This one is surrounded
by art and colors that play into
the "boho Gothic" theme.

CAN WE TALK?
The sitting room at one end of the kitchen is a cozy and intimate space, perfect for a little chat. A decoupage coffee table pairs with re-covered velvet furnishings.

Floral patterns in the rug tie into Bell's artificial plants and flowers. She finds many at IKEA.

Butcher-block counters, laminate tile floors and a white farmhouse sink keep the black in check.

A series of decorative Chinese panels ensure the kitchen is as dazzling as the other rooms.

Beyond the paint, the starting point for the look Bell desired was her art. "I collect portraits: predominately female and, if I spot one, pre-Raphaelite in style," she explains. "Everything is framed and, as often as not, every frame is spray-painted a metallic gold." Bell finds the dark walls make a great gallery for her vast collection as well as her adventurous color choices in rugs, velvet throw pillows, silk lampshades and floral bedding. Hot pinks, regal purples and lapis blues take on new roles as a cast of jewel-toned characters against each room's dark backdrop.

"I believe your sense of color is like a muscle that needs to be exercised to develop," says Bell. She advises: Be brave and follow your best instincts.

Taking inspiration for dark walls and bold hues from edgy London designer Abigail Ahern when you live in a small seaside village in Northern Ireland has a transformative effect on your home, to say the least. The results are exciting, magical and slightly disorienting. There is a definite "Wait, where am I?" effect. Look outside and you are confronted by sea, sand and sky. Inside you are transported to another time and place.

"Living here is a joy," Bell asserts of their seaside locale. "It is such a great community; a lot of artists and creative people live on our street. And everything you need is within walking distance in the village." Known as Northern Ireland's version of "Notting Hill on Sea," the beach lies almost right outside the Bells' front door.

As with much of the Irish coast and countryside, the area is popular with film crews. (Actress Sienna Miller rented the house from the previous owners while she was working in the area.) Despite that feather in its cap, the idiosyncratic house took a long time to sell. "I believe in the law of attraction, and I truly believe it was meant for us," Bell notes.

Her husband's office, a small recording studio, sits in the garden. "His passion and profession is

GATHERING PLACE
An extensive bar set behind glass, a trio of enamel pendant lights, and water views from the dining table are a few highlights of the lovely kitchen.

STAYING POWER
Guests do not easily end their visit with Bell after being treated to this sumptuous bedroom and four-poster bed.

music," so he doesn't mind having "zero input into the design," she says, laughing. "He does not interfere. It is definitely not a joint effort!"

Pulling off a rare duality, the home is child-friendly as well as elegant. "I keep valuable items out of the kids' reach for sure, but honestly, most of the furniture is upcycled out of junk shops," Bell says. She wouldn't have it otherwise.

In considering her standing ovation–worthy home, Bell encourages others to go ahead and take the dark décor plunge, a top 2021 trend. "Paint it dark: walls, woodwork, everything. And don't panic!" she says of the startling but thrilling initial results. "It looks dreadful at first, but once you have your furniture and artwork back in, it leaps into life."

 @interior_alchemy

One print propped in the window adds privacy (opposite) while another sits atop the beadboard.

UNDER FOOT
Patterned rugs are one of Bell's design staples. Those in pink and purple add romance in rooms with darker paint.

"I believe your sense of color is like a muscle that needs to be exercised."

Peggy Bell

SOAK IN SPLENDOR
Railings by Farrow & Ball meets gold frames, taps and bathtub feet. "I know it is a bit over-the-top for a bathroom!" Bell says.

159

CHAPTER 3

MAKE IT YOURS

Turn flea market finds into personal treasures with DIY tips.

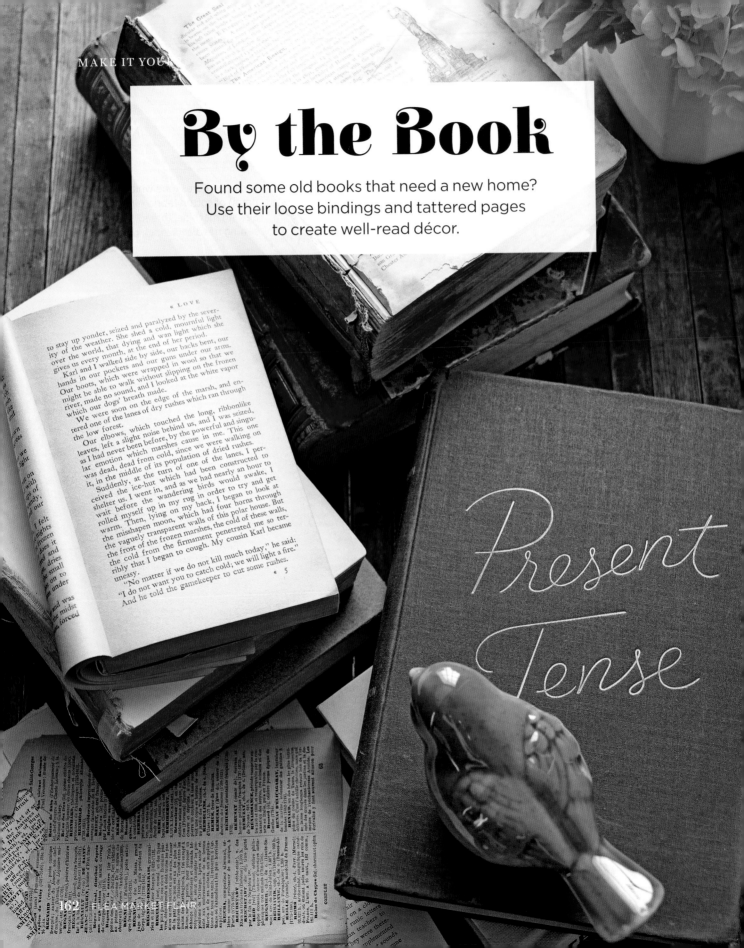

By the Book

Found some old books that need a new home?
Use their loose bindings and tattered pages
to create well-read décor.

Present Tense

The Project... **Voluminous Pillow**

A yellowed-with-age book page provides the image on this pillow.

What You'll Need
• Computer scan of book page
• Iron-on transfer paper • Two 13-inch squares (one white; one floral) of cotton fabric • Iron • Sewing machine, thread, hand-sewing needle • 12-inch pillow form

What You'll Do
1 Enlarge scan to about 8 inches square; flip image in a photo program to reverse image. Print on transfer paper.

2 Place paper facedown on white fabric; iron transfer onto fabric, following manufacturer's directions.

3 Place fabric squares with outsides facing in; stitch around three sides and four corners. Turn inside out; insert pillow form and hand-stitch opening closed.

The Project... **Storied Vase Cover**

Laced-together covers form a centerpiece for lovers of vintage volumes.

What You'll Need
• Two old books • Pencil and ruler
• Hand drill • Jute twine

What You'll Do
1 Remove any pages still attached to binding.

2 Measure and mark placement for holes evenly spaced along front edge of each cover. Drill a hole at each mark.

3 Lace the covers together on both sides with jute twine. Tie knots on the inside of the covers to hold them together. Stand the covers up in a square shape and place on a table or shelf.

The Project... **Novel Artwork**

Even beat-up books may have beautiful interiors that shine as eye-catching art.

What You'll Need
• Selection of matching or coordinating frames
• Vintage book illustrations
• Dark wax or glaze

What You'll Do
1 Select a group of illustrations. Choosing from a single book source should ensure that the images coordinate well together.

2 Place the images in frames. Unify a group of old frames by painting them a matching color.

3 Give them a vintage patina with a coat of dark wax or glaze.

The Project... **Just Your Type Photo**

Make a new snapshot feel like a family heirloom with a layer of to-the-letter patina.

What You'll Need
• Inkjet printer • Book page • Photograph • Picture frame

What You'll Do

1 In a photo-editing program, adjust the size of your photo to match as closely as possible to the size of your book page. If it's a color photo, change it to black and white. (Print a test image on regular printer paper to verify size/placement.)

2 When you're satisfied with the test image, print the photo onto the book page.

3 Place the image in a pretty frame.

No cheese here! Family photos instantly infuse a home with soul and substance.

A mirror that's propped up (as opposed to hung) lends homey casualness.

The Project... **Storied Mirror**

Give a simple mirror frame artistic status with a coating of scraps of book pages. This is a great way to use even the most battered books to create an heirloom piece.

What You'll Need
• Old book pages • Foam paintbrush • Mod Podge (gloss finish) • Any size mirror frame

What You'll Do
1 Tear the book pages into small pieces.

2 Brush Mod Podge onto one piece, place it on the frame and press to adhere. Continue adding pieces until frame is covered.

3 Brush two more coats of Mod Podge over entire frame, letting dry after each coat.

The Project... **Page-Turning Lampshade**

Cover a plain-Jane lampshade with timeworn pages that layer the lamp in texture and type.

What You'll Need
• Drum (or shallow drum) lampshade • Book pages slightly longer than lampshade • Double-sided tape • Glue gun

What You'll Do

1 Accordion-fold each page evenly and tape pages together using double-sided tape.

2 Using the glue gun, tack the pages onto the shade. Work gently if your paper is brittle. (Use pages made of thicker paper for a sturdier lampshade.)

DIY to Try Now

Trendy floral furniture transfers layered on old pieces
are a match made in a romantic-crafter's heaven.

COMING UP ROSES
This lowboy was part of a
three-piece vintage bedroom
set Denise Zdziennicki of
Salvaged Inspirations found at
an estate sale—ideal for this
Rose Celebration transfer.

Start a floral transfer design on the top of a piece, then wrap it around the front.

PICK A SIDE
The ladies of Flipping Fabulous saw the potential for big impact in this small desk, which only called for a transfer on one half.

You've seen them and you've admired them. But have you tried transfers? Maybe you've been intimidated about your skill level, unsure of the time and cost involved, or worried you don't have a piece of furniture that is glamorous enough to wear one of these instant, rub-on gardens in full bloom. But perfection isn't necessarily the goal behind the variety of floral décor transfers produced by Re-Design With Prima. In fact, even impatient or I'm-good-with-good-enough DIYers can find gratification in the fairly straightforward (and actually fun) process of smoothing these on to hide flaws on thrifted furnishings. Enliven shabby pieces or brighten any room with designs that range from sleek and sophisticated to farmhouse fresh.

Floral designs aren't the only transfers the company releases each season—they just happen to be a crowd-pleaser. Most transfers come in under $30; the very large ones are less than $50. If your piece is ready to go, you can flip your old table, desk, bed, armoire, dresser, nightstand, mirror or bookcase into a fabulous floral beauty queen in a matter of minutes. If you need more convincing that these are your new BFFs of crafting bliss, this roundup of recent furniture makeover projects certainly might do the trick.

Hints of leopard print and metallic gold glam up this table by T's Essential Inspirations.

Pieces of Prima Marketing's Rose & Rouge transfer were used here on the headboard and footboard.

"These are the best transfers on the
market, with the best selection."

Roz Robertson, New Old Finds

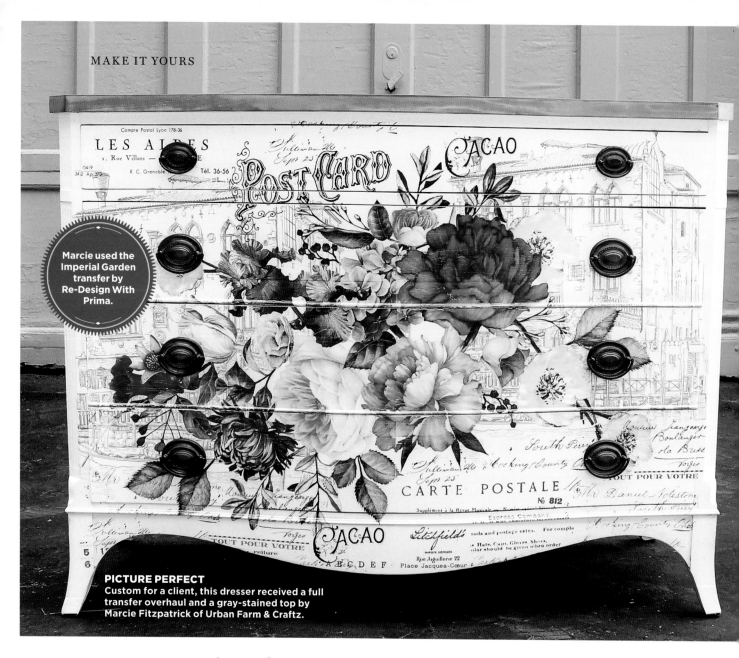

Marcie used the Imperial Garden transfer by Re-Design With Prima.

PICTURE PERFECT
Custom for a client, this dresser received a full transfer overhaul and a gray-stained top by Marcie Fitzpatrick of Urban Farm & Craftz.

5 Tips for Your First Transfer

1 Choose Your Canvas
Apply to stained, painted or raw-wood furniture. Make sure paint has dried for at least 48 hours before applying a transfer.

2 Cut to Fit
If you're using only part of the full transfer sheet, just cut out the sections you need and save the rest for another project down the road.

3 Trick for Drawers
Denise Zdziennicki of Salvaged Inspirations has a smart hack for adding transfers to the fronts of drawers (as seen on her pink lowboy project on page 168):

Remove knobs or handles, then lay the entire piece of furniture on its back on the floor. Place the transfer right over the drawer openings, rub it on using the included tool, and use a craft knife to cleanly cut the transfer between the drawer slits. Much simpler.

4 Rub and Peel
Transfers have a white backing and adhere to a plastic top sheet. Remove the backing and rub the design on, then peel back the top sheet.

5 Finish
Be patient: Wait a day or two before applying any wax or clear topcoats.

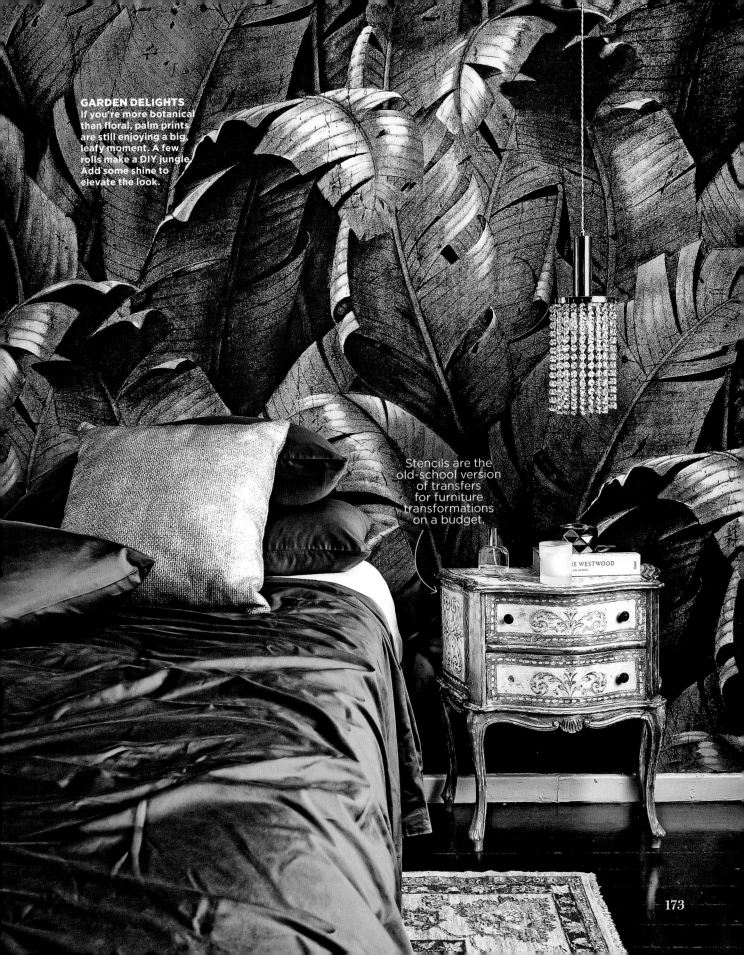

GARDEN DELIGHTS.
If you're more botanical
than floral, palm prints
are still enjoying a big,
leafy moment. A few
rolls make a DIY jungle.
Add some shine to
elevate the look.

Stencils are the
old-school version
of transfers
for furniture
transformations
on a budget.

173

From Found to Finished

Grab your tools and supplies and prepare for gratification.

Map Chair
Sitting on top of the world

"These map chairs are really easy to make for very little cost," says Claire Armstrong of pillarboxblue.com. "These are also extra special, as I made them with maps that have great sentimental meaning." She used a Norwegian street map on one to represent her husband's heritage; a Hong Kong map on another because, she shares, "I was born and brought up there" and "having lived, studied and worked" in London, she used a map of the Underground on a third. Secondhand wooden chairs team up with paper maps, glue and spray-varnish to seal. Could they be easier? If your map is very creased and worn, embrace its character—or, as Claire did on her London chair here, use gift wrap with a map print.

Found

A map gives a vintage wood chair—or even a school desk—a sense of place.

How to Make It

1 Dismantle the chairs as much as possible. (Don't worry if yours can't be taken apart, but it'll be easier if you can.)

2 Lightly sand the wooden seat and back. Use a damp microfiber cloth to carefully wipe off the dust.

3 Cut sections of the maps about 1 inch larger than the seat and back all around.

4 Brush an even coat of Elmer's glue, Mod Podge or another clear-drying PVA glue on the seat.

5 Center the seat section of map on the wooden seat so the edges extend evenly. Use a small wallpaper roller or the edge of a credit card to smooth map from center to edges to remove any air bubbles. Cut slits along map edges to make it easier to wrap around seat edges. Brush glue on seat underside and smooth down paper edges. Repeat Steps 4 and 5 for the chair back. (Note: You'll be covering any screw holes in the wood in these steps.)

6 Let glue dry, then brush another coat of glue over the maps; let dry overnight. Apply an acrylic varnish spray to all surfaces; let dry according to manufacturer's directions.

7 When all sections are completely dry, locate the screw holes and pierce through the map at each hole. Reassemble the chair.

Get All the Project Details *pillarboxblue.com/how-to-make-personalised-map-chairs*

Finished

Wouldn't a pair of these make the best wedding gift, done up in maps from the couple's home states?

Leopard Shoes
Bring out your inner animal

Found

"I love anything leopard print, especially on shoes!" says Cintia Gonzalez, the cheerful maker behind the My Poppet blog out of Australia. "So when Mum was clearing out her wardrobe and unearthed a pair of rust-stained linen shoes that happened to fit me, I had an idea." Using chalk paint and paint markers, her newly fierce shoes came to life with a roar. "I've been pattern-clashing with leopard print for years, and I don't intend to stop once the trend wanes. It seems to go with everything."

Finished

How to Make It

1 Stir to mix Annie Sloan Chalk Paint in Barcelona Orange or shade of your choice.

2 Pour a small amount into a jar. Add an equal amount of water. Stir well so it's runny but still opaque. The paint should soak into the fabric like a wash or stain, not coat it. If it's too thick, it may crack or crease once it dries.

3 Ensure shoes are clean, dry and dust-free. Remove laces. If there are areas of the shoes you don't want to paint, like the soles here, tape them off.

4 Using a dabbing brush, apply a thin coat of paint over both shoes. Wipe off any excess. Allow to dry thoroughly.

5 Find an online image of "leopard print design" as inspiration, and practice painting it on paper first. (Cintia used a black-and-white one with gold highlights.)

6 Starting at the heel, use a white paint marker (Pilot makes a good one) to place random splotches on shoes. Don't make the shapes too even. Allow ink to dry before moving to the next color to prevent bleeding or smudging.

7 Add black details over white markings. Refer back to your image to keep the design on track. Once dry, add gold highlights, if desired.

8 Use a stiff-bristle brush to dab on Annie Sloan Clear Wax or a natural shoe polish to seal.

Get All the Project Details *mypoppet.com.au/makes/leopard-print-chalk-paint-shoe-makeover*

Found

Finished

Papered Bureau
Go mad for plaid

This masculine and sophisticated mahogany dresser by Brandy Kollenborn of the Brushed by Brandy blog and Etsy shop was inspired by an English library and Victorian smoking room. She envisioned a cigar lounge with leather chairs, plaid wallpaper and hunting-scene artwork. The piece took four weeks to complete in her Sacramento, California, studio, but the result is second to none. "These three-drawer chests are some of my favorite to work on," Brandy shares. "Their classic style and moderate size make them great for just about any space: an entryway, sofa table, media center or accent piece. I pick them up every time!"

How to Make It

1 For best results, use heavyweight, satin-finish, plaid-print gift wrap. Remove all of the chest front's hardware.

2 Strip any paint or finish from the top. Clean dresser with Dixie Belle White Lightning Cleaner. Sand any rough or damaged areas until smooth.

3 Apply a coat of Dixie Belle B.O.S.S., a stain- and odor-blocking primer.

4 On the top, apply Dixie Belle Voodoo gel stain in Tobacco Road.

5 On the rest of the chest, apply two coats of Dixie Belle paint in Caviar. (Brandy added a bit of Palmetto paint for the sides, to tie in with the greens from the paper.) Let dry.

6 Cut paper to fit each drawer front. Apply wallpaper paste to fronts and papers; press paper in place and smooth with a brayer.

7 Wax drawer glides. Apply copper gilding wax to legs. Seal paper with Dixie Belle Gator Hide clear coat.

8 Clean hardware, then coat with copper spray paint, followed by a wash of the Caviar paint to highlight details. Follow with more clear coat. Reattach all hardware.

Get All the Project Details *brushedbybrandy.com/2019/07/22/plaid-gentlemans-chest*

Kristy Robb of robbrestyle.com fell for this chair the moment she spotted it in a local thrift shop. "I loved the seashell-like shape of the back. But the fabric was a faded pea-green brocade, and I knew this kind of reupholstery was beyond my skill set." Given her penchant for painting—and the craze for DIY fabric painting—she decided to take a risk with this no-fuss method, since the fabric was in good shape. "The key to painting upholstery is to choose a low-nap fabric," Kristy says. "I wanted this project to be effortless, so I didn't remove the nailheads. I simply painted over them generously and wiped away the excess paint with a damp cloth. I love that this paint finish has a little sheen to it once dry. It looks elegant and finished. And I didn't have to do any extra prepping or adjust the paint with fabric medium or water. I just painted it on!"

How to Make It

1 Bring the furniture outdoors for the best ventilation.

2 Using a brush, apply Velvet Finishes by Kellie Smith paint in Baroque in two coats, pressing the brush to get into the grooves of the fabric.

3 When completely dry, apply a very light-grit sandpaper across the surface to achieve a smooth, leatherlike finish.

Get All the Project Details
robbrestyle.com/no-fuss-diy-chair-paint

Found

Painted Armchair
Yes, it's OK to color upholstery!

Finished

Decorated Purse

Everyone loves a polka-dot bag

Found

Finished

How to Make It

1 Stuff the purse with rags. Lightly rub the surface with fine grit sandpaper (220) to remove the shiny treatment on the leather and allow the upcoming dye to soak into the leather.

2 Use a damp cloth to wipe off sanding dust.

3 Wearing rubber gloves, use a foam brush to apply thin coats of Tandy's Eco-Flo All-in-One (dye and finish; Lauren used black), applying light pressure to the brush as you go.

4 Create a stencil for your pattern. (Lauren used a Silhouette Cameo electronic cutting tool.) Secure the stencil to the purse with rubber bands.

5 Use a dabber brush and Plaids' FolkArt Metallic Acrylic paint in Gold to paint dots through the stencil. Keep stencil pressed flat; use multiple thin coats.

6 Remove stencil. Clean up any stray strokes with a little black dye on a tiny brush to disguise them.

auren Lanker of thinkingcloset.com inherited this vintage black purse when a beloved family friend passed away. "I can't remember a holiday meal during my childhood when Ruth wasn't at our table, warming us with her smiling eyes and clever quips," she says of the purse's original owner. But the purse was showing its age. "I knew she would be proud I had given her purse a new lease on life."

Get All the Project Details thinkingcloset.com/purse

Matching Tables
Separate pieces become twins

Found

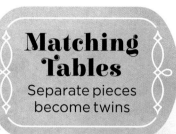

Vintage tables are harder to find in sets than as singles. But sometimes you need a pair! Furniture and home décor painting artist Sara Hollister-Jessick of Surrey Lane Home found one of these two round tables with front doors at a local resale shop, then stashed it away for six months until she found the other in a very similar size and shape. The new twinning pink tables sold at Then and Now Antique and Consignment House in Petoskey, Michigan, where she consigns her work.

How to Make It

1 Clean tables with soap and water. Let dry. Remove the hardware.

2 Apply two coats of Annie Sloan Chalk Paint in Antoinette, letting dry after each coat.

3 Slightly distress the table finish with sandpaper to your own liking.

4 Follow directions to seal with Annie Sloan Clear Wax.

5 Switch out original brass hardware with new or vintage glass knobs, if desired.

Get All the Project Details
instagram.com/surrey_lane_home

Finished

Finished

Found

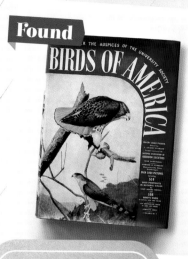

Wall Prints
Vintage birds make great art

Kindrel Murchison and her husband, Warren, are renovating their 1979 fixer-upper one project at a time. After cutting and adding 9.5-inch-wide plywood strips to their walls for a plank look, Murchison began dreaming of this flora-meets-fauna art wall. It's so simple, it almost doesn't need instruction!

"I used vintage pants hangers that I've collected over the years (I sell vintage and handmade home décor locally) because I loved the varying wood tones, which complement my vintage farmhouse-inspired home really well," she says. "The bird prints are carefully cut out of my beloved vintage *Birds of America* book." She mapped out the grid on her living room floor first to ensure a visually balanced layout. With the help of a tall ladder, the pair worked carefully from the top to the bottom, hanging each print row by row, using 1-inch nails. "The hangers are different heights, so we had to go by eye, and what looked good as a whole, when setting up each individual print," she adds.

Get All the Project Details
instagram.com/lovelyhomebykj

Vinyled Stove
Give your oven some lovin'

Found

A dated stove that's short on good looks is a prime candidate for vinyl.

The talented Ashley Wilson of At Home With Ashley had admired the work of fellow crafty bloggers who had applied car vinyl to their appliances. She decided to give it a go and introduce some retro color in her own kitchen. "The stove was old and came with our house," she says. "It was boring and dated but works great. So I'm happy the pink update made it much cuter!" The Utah-based mom tackled the door in about an hour. "The vinyl can withstand heat up to 400 degrees, making it safer than most paint," she adds.

How to Make It

1 Order two 24-by-60 sheets of pink car vinyl—or more, depending on the size of the area you want to cover.

2 Remove the door handle and clean the stove really well to avoid bubbles.

3 Starting at the door's upper edge, stick the top of the vinyl onto the door so it extends a couple of inches on each side. Use a squeegee to smooth it out.

4 Use a blow dryer to seal the vinyl in place. Pull off the backing an inch at a time, then blow heat onto that section with the dryer. Use a squeegee to smooth out every inch. Repeat along the entire front.

5 If you get a crease or bubble, pull up the vinyl, reheat it with the blow dryer and reapply.

6 Work quickly: The vinyl gets tackier as it sits.

7 Cut the vinyl on the sides to the door's depth; heat and smooth it as in Step 4. Trim the excess using the snake razor blade included with the vinyl.

Get All the Project Details *athomewithashley.com/how-to-wrap-an-oven*

Finished

Candy pink is
a throwback
contrast to
Ashley's mint
green cupboards,
while keeping
the same vibe.

Top Shelf
Half a hutch finds new life

Found

Finished

" love hutches, especially in kitchens—so I was pretty bummed when we moved in and I saw that we had no room for one in our eating area," says Nashville, Tennessee-based Carissa Brown, creator of the Bless This Nest blog. When she found an outdated top hutch piece at a yard sale for $25, she felt like she had hit the jackpot. "It was way past its glory days," she says, which inspired its farmhouse-style, chalk paint redo. And hanging it on the wall allowed just enough room for her kitchen table and chairs.

How to Make It

1 Have a piece of wood custom-cut to fit across the bottom of the hutch to form a shelf.

2 Remove the hutch's hardware (knobs, hinges, etc.) and the glass from the hutch's doors.

3 Paint both the hutch and the wood piece with Annie Sloan Pure White Chalk Paint; let dry, then apply a coat of clear wax.

4 Cut chicken wire to fit the openings where the glass was removed; attach in place.

5 Screw the shelf to the hutch bottom.

6 Replace the old knobs. (Carissa's came from Hobby Lobby.)

7 Locate wall studs and carefully mount the hutch with heavy-duty screws.

Get All the Project Details *blessthisnestblog.com/2017/06/04/outdated-hutch-makeover*

Found

Finished

While some DIYers have put their vintage card catalogs on wheels to create low tables, Deborah McDonald of B Vintage Style had loftier plans for hers. "The library cabinet was previously used in a workshop as a toolbox. It was extremely heavy and full of really big tools," she recalls. When she sourced an antique washstand, she knew she had a match that she could stack together to create extra storage. "Although I was nervous to paint this piece," she confesses, "I'm so happy with how it turned out." The bottom cabinet holds printer and designer samples for her business, Vintage Society Co., while she actually uses the top to hold wine! Bottles fit perfectly in the drawers.

How to Make It

1 Lightly sand all the pieces down before you paint them.

2 "Canadian Tire [a paint company] had approached me to collaborate with them on its color of the month at that time, which was Gold Champagne, so I thought that it would be a good time to pick this as my project piece," Deborah says. "I needed to use just two coats of the Canadian Tire Premier paint—the coverage is excellent."

3 Lightly sand the edges of both pieces with a mouse sander to get a distressed look.

4 Apply antiquing wax according to package directions.

5 Stack pieces together. (For added stability, consider securing them together on the back using brackets, or fastening to the wall, if necessary.)

Get All the Project Details vintagesocietyco.com/one-of-a-kind-diy-antique-storage-cabinet

CREDITS

COVER www.timeincukcontent.com **2-3** Ely Fair Photography; Daniel Mathis/Instagram @notaminimalist **4-5** Yudina Elena/Shutterstock; Nicole Mertz/Instagram @kansasgirlvintage; thinkingcloset.com/purse; Mark Lohman **6-7** Anita Diaz/Instagram whispering.pines.homestead **8-9** GAP Interiors/Light Locations **10-11** Aundrea Marie Photography **12-13** Paris Match/Getty Images; Junk in the Trunk **14-15** Melissa Urban/ Shabby Love Blog; Liz Fourez/LoveGrowsWild.com; Erin Kern/CottonStem.com; Lew Robertson/Getty Images; Jessica Wasserman/Instagram @jesswasserman **16-17** TheHumbleclub/Etsy; Cat Nguyen Photography; goseek/Etsy; Richard Powers/ArcaidImages/Getty Images; VINTAGEnfinity/Etsy **18-19** Andreas von Einsiedel/ Getty Images; Les Hirondelles/Getty Images; Paul Viant/Getty Images; Richard Powers/Arcaid Images/Getty Images; Richard Powers/Arcaid Images/Getty Images **20-21** Lance Gerber; Lee Vosburgh/StyleBee.ca; Erin Kern/CottonStem.com; Robert Nicholas/Getty Images **22-23** Colin Poole/GAP Interiors;Susan Daggett/ KindredVintageCo.com; Kristi Dominguez/IShouldBeMoppingTheFloor.com; Jessica Wasserman/Instagram @jesswasserman; Cheryl Chan/Getty images; Erin Kern/CottonStem.com **24-25** Copper Corners; Katrina Lounsbury; Ashley Gilbreath Interior Design; Andreas von Einsiedel/Getty Images; Erin Kern/CottonStem.com; Painted Cottage Prairie/Etsy **26-27** Per Magnus Persson/Getty Images; Sharon Lapkin/Getty Images; barbaracarrollphotography/Getty Images **28-29** AnyDirectFlight/Getty Images; Andreas von Einsiedel/Getty Images; Pieter Estersohn/Getty Images **30-31** Andreas von Einsiedel/Getty Images; Melanie Butcher/Instagram @vintagecharmhouse **32-33** timeincukcontent.com **34-35** Francis Dean/Shutterstock; Incamerastock/Alamy; Jodie Johnson/Shutterstock **36-37** Anna Mroszczyk/Shutterstock; RobertHarding/Alamy; Nicola Margaret/ Getty Images **38-39** Yudina Elena/Shutterstock; Pierre-Yves Babelon/Getty Images; Steve Sparrow/Getty Images **40-41** Light Locations/GAP Interiors; Daisy Corlett/Alamy; GVictoria/Shutterstock; Salvator Barki/ Getty; Beren Patterson/Alamy **42-43** Sorendels/Getty Images; Encyclopedia Britannica/UIG/Getty Images **44-45** Mark Lohman **46-53** Nicole Campbell/Erice-Marie Photography **54-61** Anita Diaz/Instagram @whispering.pines.homestead **62-69** Nicole Mertz/Instagram @kansasgirlvintage **70-77** Chelsi Gobeil/ Instagram @gobeil_soleil **78-87** Mark Lohman **88-99** Mark Lohman **100-109** Nicole Mertz/Instagram @kansasgirlvintage **110-119** Mary Vitullo/Instagram @orphanswithmakeup **120-129** Photography by Robin Stubbert/GAP Interiors **130-139** Mark Lohman **140-149** Jenasie Earl/Instagram @msviciousdesign; @megosburnphoto **150-159** GAP Interiors/Douglas Gibb **160-161** PhotoAttractive/Getty Images **162-167** GAP Interiors/Caruth Studi **168-169** Denise Zdziennicki of SalvagedInspirations.com; Flippingfabuloussalina.com **170-171** Instagram @Tsessentialinspirations; New Old Finds by Roz Robertson/Instagram @newoldfinds **172-173** Instagram @urbanfarmandcraftz; Bureaux/GAP Interiors **174-175** Claire Armstrong/PillarBoxBlue. com **176-177** Cintia Gonzalez/mypoppet.com/au; Brandy Kollenborn/brushedbybrandy.com **178-179** Kristy Robb/robbrestyle.com; Lauren Lanker/thinkingcloset.com **180-181** Sara Hollister-Jessick/Instagram @surrey_ lane_home; Kindrel Juliet/Instagram @lovelyhomebykj **182-183** Ashley Wilson/Instagram @athomewithashley **184-185** Carissa Brown/Instagram @bless_this_nest; Deborah McDonald/vintagesocietyco.com **BACK COVER** Mark Lohman

---

SPECIAL THANKS TO CONTRIBUTING WRITER

Fifi O'Neill

CENTENNIAL BOOKS

An Imprint of
Centennial Media, LLC
40 Worth St., 10th Floor
New York, NY 10013, U.S.A.

ISBN 978-1-951274-59-7

Distributed by
Simon & Schuster, Inc.
1230 Avenue of the Americas
New York, NY 10020, U.S.A.

For information about custom editions, special sales and premium and corporate purchases, please contact Centennial Media at contact@centennialmedia.com.

Manufactured in China

Publishers & Co-Founders Ben Harris, Sebastian Raatz
Editorial Director Annabel Vered
Creative Director Jessica Power
Executive Editor Janet Giovanelli
Features Editor Alyssa Shaffer
Deputy Editors Ron Kelly, Anne Marie O'Connor
Design Director Martin Elfers
Senior Art Director Pino Impastato
Art Directors Runyon Hall, Natali Suasnavas, Joseph Ulatowski
Copy/Production Patty Carroll, Angela Taormina
Assistant Art Director Jaclyn Loney
Photo Editor Jenny Veiga
Production Manager Paul Rodina
Production Assistant Alyssa Swiderski
Editorial Assistant Tiana Schippa
Sales & Marketing Jeremy Nurnberg